SHACK

THE LIFE, TIMES AND LEGACY OF LEN SHACKLETON

Possibly the most naturally talented footballer ever to play in England

E T Laing

Copyright © E T Laing

E T Laing was born in Northern Ireland and spent his childhood in the North East of England. He now lives in London with his family and works mainly for the international aid agencies. His recent travel book, "Fakirs, Feluccas and Femmes Fatales", was based on the seventy countries he has worked in.

With particular thanks to Carola Groom, Ray Kershaw and Rob Mason for their suggestions, editing, fact checking and support.

Published by Penthesilea Books

23 Roderick Road
London NW3 2NN

2016

ISBN no. 978-1-326-60245-1

Printed by lulu.com

Front cover photograph with permission from Shutterstock

The author has made all reasonable efforts to contact copyright holders of photographs for permission and apologises for any omissions

CONTENTS

1.	Shack: The Centre Of Our Small World In The North East	5
2.	Overview of his Career	12
3.	The North East After The War	21
4.	Roker Park: A Saturday Afternoon In The 1950s	27
5.	Just How Good Was He?	35
6.	His Three Clubs	40
7.	Football And Social Class	47
8.	The Maximum Wage	55
9.	Shack's Nine Years At Sunderland	61
10.	His International Career	68
11.	The Secret of His Success	74
12.	The Footballers Turn To Crime	78
13.	The Book	83
14.	Reactions To The Book	93
15.	What Was He Like: Clown Or Devil?	96
16.	His Footballing Twin In Brazil	105
17.	His Later Years	114
18.	The End Of The Maximum Wage	119
19.	The End Of The English Footballers' Contract	132
20.	Freedom At Last: The Bosman Ruling And Consequences	153
21.	What Became of the Players who Pushed for Reforms?	162
22.	The State Of English Football Today	172
23.	Summing Him Up	186

1
Shack:
The Centre of Our Small World in the North East

2015

The journalists waiting outside the airport for the plane to Madrid can hear the crowd starting to buzz, and know that the team bus must have arrived. They turn and there it is, like a spaceship, its glaring halogen headlights reflecting through the drizzle off the seal-black tarmac. The well-known faces are just about visible in the dim lights behind the tinted windows as it glides to a stop in a heavily policed area. The crowd presses forward. The door opens and the demi-gods troop down the steps. The rich may or may not be different from you and me, but the rich footballer is different in a different way, as if from a distant planet. The journalists, wordsmiths all, pull out their notebooks and ransack their vocabularies and memories for killer similes – coil-sprung thoroughbreds, sleek snow leopards, perfumed panthers, silent assassins, pampered princelings. The footballers look somehow military in their blue blazers, like praetorian guards, as the flashbulbs pop and the camera shutters snap, snap, snap. Their minders hurry them on into the VIP lounge and out of sight. The crowd, which had grown much bigger, now subsides. The journalists take out their economy class tickets and head for the check-in.

* * *

It was not always like this. Not in 1944 when one of the greatest footballers who ever lived looked exactly like what he was at the age of twenty two: a runty little coal miner, with the oiled, side parted hair you see in World War II photos. Len Shackleton had to wait another year for the war to end before he became a professional footballer on £8 a week and later went on to play for England. He ended his career on the maximum basic wage of £17 – which was less than my starting salary in an office only a few years later.

Shack was the shining star at the centre of the small world of my post-war childhood, in which there was little apart from school, football, cricket and children's hour on the radio.

He joined Sunderland in 1948, just two years before my long allegiance to the team was settled one evening after choir practice. We, the sopranos, had made our routine diversion on the way home from the church - to terrorise Miss Sadie's Dancing Class. The class was held every week in a basement further down the main road, where, from street level, we could see, through the window, the nice smartly-dressed young boys and girls in their shiny dancing shoes learning to foxtrot. We lined up, bent down and shouted our usual taunt.

"Sissies."

Miss Sadie turned, glared up at us and ran to the window, shaking her fist and mouthing:

"I know who you are ….."

We made silly faces and turned to run.

But this time I found that I could not move. My arm had been twisted behind my back, the steely grip was tightening and a very hard and unknown voice behind my ear said:

"Who do you support, kidder, Sunderland or Newcastle?"

The consequences of the wrong choice were unthinkable. I panicked, but grabbed at the thought that our village was eight miles from Newcastle and only four from Sunderland.

"Er …Sunderland."

It turned out to be the right answer, and I was sent on my way with a grudging kick.

The following year I started to go to Roker Park, having reached a height at which I could see about a quarter of the game. My father took me the first time, but I think he might have considered football rather common. Anyway, after that I was on my own; and every alternate Saturday after lunch I could be found waiting hopefully at the bus stop to Sunderland - an hour too early, on the off chance of catching one of the ten or so buses that sped past full of supporters, until I despaired and ran the three miles to the ground.

Arriving drenched in sweat, I joined the queue to pay my one shilling and three pence, then pushed through the clanking cast iron turnstile and ran round past the concrete bunker smelling of beer and urine that was the toilet. If there was time I bought a pie filled with liquid meat and tomato sauce, then climbed up the steps and down into a crowd of, often, over 60,000 men in dun coloured raincoats and flat caps. (Only on Boxing Day was there an injection of colour, from the 20,000 yellow scarves the men had been given as Christmas presents by their wives). I made my way down to the front where the other boys I knew usually stood, and if it was crowded the adults would pick us up and pass us over the top on to the straw laid out around the pitch – just as the brass band that played before the game was trooping off.

And there I was, at the centre of the known universe - my heartbeat thudding against my ribs after the long run.

Roker Park was the only place I have ever felt truly, truly part of a crowd. The atoms of which I am composed react weakly in crowds, even on New Year's Eve or at a carnival or a rally. But the anticipation on those winter afternoons in the quarter hour before the game started, as we stamped our feet and rubbed our mittens together to keep warm ... ah, that was something different.

Sunderland was the only team never to have been out of the First Division, and was known as the "Bank of England" team. It was the Chelsea or Manchester City of the 1950s, spending high "buy" success. They had spent a quarter of a million pounds on players from outside the north east, many of them glamorous internationals who were beginning to be distinguishable from the stocky figures with brylcreemed hair parted in the middle and eyes close together that made up the average team. One actually owned a car.

But despite the stellar line up Sunderland's results could be grindingly disappointing. They specialised in dismal 1-1 draws, played out doggedly on foggy afternoons on pitches that were, by November, more mud than grass. The pattern was often the same. We took the lead with an early goal and at half time, when the stands opposite winked in the darkness as ten thousand cigarettes lit up, our expectations were high. They rose even higher as the floodlights - still glamorous to us – were switched on and the players trooped out for the second half. But what I remember most of all is the fog thickening after half time, the floodlights looking hazy and dim in the damp air, the soggy leather ball slithering to a stop in the mud, the missed chances, and the resigned groans at the visiting team's late equalizer or winner - which we reluctantly clapped (yes, we did: we were also careful not to be too triumphalist when we scored.)

What Sunderland did have, though, was Shack, the ex-Bevin Boy[1] with unprepossessing looks, borderline lazy in his later years - but with ball control that was unsurpassed.

Before he arrived at Sunderland in 1948, Shack had already made his name at Sunderland's arch enemy, Newcastle United, where he scored six goals in his debut - a record breaking 13-0 win against Newport. He then moved to Sunderland for the highest ever transfer fee of £20,050 (of which he received nothing); and for the next ten years he monopolised the thoughts of a town. We loved Shack immediately and unconditionally for his comment after he left Newcastle for Sunderland:

"I'm not biased against Newcastle. I don't care who beats them."

He couldn't have chosen a better opening line. In my village close to Sunderland there were grown men who would not eat a black and white sweet.

His style was from a lost age. Think for a moment of the spectacle of Diego Costa scoring a goal today – the cocktail of adrenaline and testosterone pumping dangerously in the veins

---

[1] Bevin Boys were men who worked in the coal mines during the Second World War, named after the Minister of Labour and National Service, Ernest Bevin.

in his forehead. Well, this is what Shack was like: after dribbling round a full-back, he would stop, put his foot on the ball, flick his shirt sleeve back and mime looking at his watch; or, after beating another back, he would mime lifting a cup off a saucer and having a sip of tea. One afternoon, at Highbury, he stopped and sat down on the ball. The players asked if he was alright, and Shack assured them he was fine – before standing up slowly and running through the defence to score before they knew what was happening.

Some of the other greats didn't like it. Stanley Matthews, who was almost as skilful as Shack, was reported to have disapproved of making fun of an opponent; and Trevor Ford, Sunderland's centre forward and the most expensive player in the country (with a transfer fee of £30,000), eventually went as far as refusing to play with the unpredictable Shack. He claimed, correctly, that Shack derived malicious satisfaction from imparting a vicious spin to what seemed like perfect passes, to make Ford look clumsy in front of the crowd. On one occasion Shack dribbled through a whole defence, to reach the goal line and then turned to tap the ball back to Ford, shouting to the crowd, "You can't say I never pass to you." After that they often played on their own in alternate matches, until Ford was eventually sold, and ended back in his home town of Cardiff.

The Times' obituary for Shack said that "everyone who ever saw him play has a favourite Shackleton story ... he was almost guaranteed to provide something out of the ordinary on every appearance". One of mine was from the first floodlit game I saw, when he took the ball on the half way line and juggled it from head to instep to thigh to chest until it hit the back of the net - without having touched the ground. Another was the time he kicked the ball down the pitch, ambled forward to circle round the full back challenging him, and trapped it neatly as it came back to him like a boomerang, albeit in a strong wind.

But it was not those one-off performances that were the most memorable: it was the magic of his footwork week in week out. The few seconds of film of him playing that still exist are not of his greatest moments: they are just of a typical mid-game run. But they bring it all back. There he would stand, foot over the ball, eyes scanning the pitch like an Indian scout.

Then, as a defender closed in to tackle, he would sink into a low crouch, poised like a panther, tempting the defender to make his move. The defender would dart forward and suddenly Shack would be erect like a skier at the top of his turn, before dipping and - with rocket booster acceleration - setting out on his mazy run, past the first defender and on to the next, swaying, slowing, accelerating, and swivelling, all with the low centre of gravity of the slalom skier as he picked his way through the defence, the ball glued to his feet. Messi and Hazard are the two players that come to mind.

The dribbling was not all he had. He was one of the first to perfect the lobbed goal, which he called his mashie niblick shot after the golf iron; he could back heel at speed; and he could shoot. Malcolm Hartley the author of a history of the Bradford team where Shackleton started his career wrote that "apart from the adhesive ball control and breath-taking body swerve, Shack could hit a ball. His slender legs could crack the ball like a Bofors gun."

He retired early by the standards of those days, at 35, after an ankle injury. He then set up as a hairdresser.

We feared that he might go the same way as other footballing giants who went into sad declines – like Wilf Mannion, the blond-haired golden boy from Middlesbrough who later in life was reduced to working on building sites and trading on past fame in the pubs for another drink and a cigarette.

But Shack had brains as well as golden feet. Before he retired he had already written a serious book - "Clown Prince of Soccer" – that tore into the directors that ran England's football clubs, the niggardly maximum wage they paid and the archaic controls they imposed on the players to keep them under the thumb. The book kick-started the reforms that have transformed football into what is today.

His sense of humour was already known before he wrote his book. Of the Newport County team that Newcastle had beaten 13-0 in Shack's first game for them in 1946 he memorably told the match reporter:

"Wey, they were lucky to get nil."

And as the years passed he put his wit to good use with another book and as a journalist. Even in his sixties he was still going strong. Of the Russian team of the mid 1990s, he started a match report:

"If you thought Ivan was terrible, you should have seen this lot."

The Inland Revenue's offices in Sunderland are named Shackleton House in his honour.

2

Overview of his Career

Len Shackleton, the sporting hero of the North East, was not born there. He was born in the Yorkshire city of Bradford in 1922 and spoke with a Yorkshire accent throughout his life.

He believed that he had inherited his unusual sporting ability from his father, dedicating his first book to:

> "the memory of my father, Leonard Price Shackleton (1898-1972), an ardent amateur sportsman himself – cricketer, footballer and track athlete. It was his enthusiasm, encouragement and support that enabled me to become a professional sportsman".

But there are two puzzles here. First, while Shack was the consummate artist with a football his father was the opposite, a hard tackler who 'got stuck in' and took pride in having often been sent off. And, secondly, there is little evidence elsewhere of his father having a very supportive attitude, except for the remarkable fact that he allowed Shack to clear the furniture out of the sitting room to play football indoors on most evenings when he was young. But later, even after Shack played for England, his father showed little enthusiasm or encouragement: in fact he seems never to have given him any praise at all. After one particularly good game during the war in which Shack scored all five goals he hoped for a pat on the back when he got home. Eventually, he had to ask:

"Don't you think it was good match?"

His father just stared into the fire. There was a long pause before the reply came:

"Your sister could have back heeled another three into the net." Then a few years later Shack topped his five goal record in perhaps the most spectacular debut in English football history, when he scored six goals in his first game for Newcastle United. His father's reaction? Silence. Rather generously

Shack recalls in his book that "dad's attitude has helped me keep my feet on the ground and my head out of the clouds".

From an early age Shack was unusually gifted with an ability to play any sport with a moving ball. Later in life he was to win a tennis competition the first time he picked up a racket, mastered the rudiments of baseball in a few minutes and played cricket at county level. But in the early years it was football that consumed him.

He was never without a ball in his pocket, usually a tennis ball, which he pulled out as soon as he left the house to play, even after dark under the street lights or by the lights of the local shops. Like most families in the recession between the two wars they were poor and could not afford football boots, so his Uncle John, who wanted him to become a footballer, nailed some studs on to an old pair of shoes.

Success came early, and lasted throughout his life - first, as a footballer then as a businessman and later as a journalist and writer. But throughout the years in which he was perhaps the most famous and admired man in the north east his income – which was the maximum wage imposed by the Football League - was less than an office worker's. And in the year that he first played for England (1948) he was still working in a coal mine, alongside his mate "wor" Jackie Milburn, the other local hero whose fame rivalled Shack's.

A bright kid, he won a scholarship and was allowed a choice of grammar schools - opting for the Carlton school across town because it had the best football team. He was soon the captain of the team, scoring forty goals in fourteen matches, and began to play for Bradford Schoolboys. A school teacher then recommended him to play for the North against the Midlands schoolboys, where, at one inch under five feet, he was the smallest boy on the pitch, but he shone enough to selected for the England's schoolboys team.

An early photo shows him, looking shy, being congratulated by his school friends. He went on to score two goals in a 6-2 win against Wales and later played against Scotland and Northern Ireland.

By 14, however, he was too old to play for the schoolboy teams, as most children left school around that age in the 1930s. His next move was to join Bradford Park Avenue as an amateur. But Bradford couldn't keep him long.

In the late 1930s the best team in the country - and maybe the world - was Arsenal, who had won the league championship five times between 1930 and 1938. Another school teacher alerted them to Shack's talents. A scout was sent out to watch him, and then one evening a big car – it might have been a Rolls or a Chrysler – drew up outside 38 Soaper Lane, and the neighbours stared as George Allison, the manager of mighty Arsenal, emerged from the back seat, knocked at the door and announced that he had come all the way from London to Bradford to ask Len to join them. Shack recalled that "at that time, any 15-year-old boy, if invited to join the greatest club in the world, would have been out of his mind to think twice, and so it was that I accepted his offer of a job on the ground staff and signed as an amateur."

But, arriving in London at the age of 16, he found that his new job was not all he had been expecting. On his first day he was handed overalls but no football boots or shirt, and then loaned out to Enfield Town who played in the Athenian League. The only brush with fame that "this frail boy" - which was how a match programme described him - had in that year came a few weeks later. Arsenal's most expensive new player, Bryn Jones, had just been signed at a record fee of £14,000, and a local newspaper thought it would be amusing to show Jones's photograph with the caption "He cost £14,000" alongside a picture of Shack holding a pair of grass clippers captioned "He cost nothing".

He was paid two pounds and ten shillings (£2.50) a week, and as the months went by he had little contact with the stars.

He played for an Arsenal team only once. Then after only ten months he was summoned by Allison and told that he had not made the grade. "Go back to Bradford and get another job," said Allison. "You'll never be a footballer." Shack might well have wondered if his exit had been connected with an earlier incident when Allison, visiting the training ground, had put his shoe up on a railing and called to Shack in his affected upper class accent, "Come here, boy, and tie my shoelaces." There was never any chance that Shack, even at that age, would have considered any other reply ... "Tie them yourself," he said to the great man.

Heartbroken, he could hardly face the thought of going back to the north a failure. Just before he left Bradford a headline in a local newspaper had read "Given Big Chance by Arsenal - Bradford Ex-Schoolboy International Seeks Football Fame"; and later the same newspaper reported "Today Leonard set off on his great adventure."

But there was another boy, called Harry Ward, who has also just been rejected by Arsenal, and by a stroke of luck they were tipped off about a manager at the London Paper Mills at Dartford in east London who might offer a job to a good footballer who was willing to play for the company. Shack and his friend took a chance with the cost of the fare over there and found the kindly manager happy to take them on despite their lack of paper making skills. And there he stayed until the war was declared and he returned to Bradford.

He signed his first professional contract with Bradford Park Avenue in August 1940, and during the war he scored 166 goals for them, while working at the same time at a General Electric Company (GEC) aircraft wireless factory. While he was there he saw all his friends, one by one, enlist, and he applied for the air force and Fleet Air Arm. But he was rejected because his work was considered essential for the war effort and GEC refused to release him. Later, when the government asked men liable for conscription to volunteer to work in the mines instead of joining the forces he became a Bevin Boy[2], while continuing to play for Bradford.

Bradford, once again, couldn't keep him. As soon as the war finished he was attracting the attention of talent scouts and the club realised that he was worth a lot of money. Not that this was any of Shack's business as a player. Transfer fees were negotiated by and paid to clubs, with nothing going to the player, who was a passive figure in the transaction. Nor did a transfer mean a higher wage, as both clubs - the buyers as well as the sellers – imposed the same maximum wage. In fact when he was summoned one evening to a hotel in the middle of Bradford Shack was not even aware that he might be sold. He only found out what was happening that evening when an unknown business man materialised in the company of his Bradford chairman, and told Shack that he would be coming to the North East. It transpired that he was Stan Seymour, a director of Newcastle United and the deal had been completed

The demeaning manner in which Shack, by this time the second most expensive footballer in England, was treated was mirrored in the transfer of Danny Blanchflower three years later and Stewart Imlach (see Chapters 7 and 13 for more details of the transfers of both players).

---

[2] See footnote in Chapter 1

His arrival at Newcastle was electrifying. They had lost their previous four games, but they won Shack's first game by a record-breaking 13-nil with Shack scoring six.

But success at this highest level did not bring great rewards. The days of manual work for footballers had not ended, and despite being the new sporting hero in an area where football was everything, and having been sold for the second highest fee ever in England, he still had to work down the mines on weekdays. In fact, he worked alongside the other superstar, Jackie Milburn, the Newcastle and England forward who was also a miner. He remembered that Shack "was my labourer at Hazelrigg workshops after I left Ashington colliery. We both had to go there because of the reserved occupation lark. I had a motorbike and we went backwards and forwards to Newcastle's ground at St James Park three times a week for training, Shack on the back, with our pit gear on". (After his eventual retirement I saw Milburn in a garden in Newcastle and found that he sold lawn mowers for a living after football).

Despite his glorious start Shack was never quite happy at Newcastle. He was irritated by the directors' meanness – they "didn't even pay for new laces" – and they did not provide him the accommodation they had promised him. Worse, his unique talent was starting to be a mixed blessing. There were rumours of friction with Newcastle's centre forward Charlie Wayman, who was not able to match Shack's quick thinking on the pitch and eventually asked for a transfer. Wayman was quoted in the Daily Mirror as saying: "Shack is a very difficult partner to play with, simply because he is so talented and it is not always easy to understand what he wants." In his second year Shack's dissatisfaction over his house and the Newcastle directors' defaulting on the promise to pay the £500 signing-on fee led him to submit a transfer request.

Then one night he answered the doorbell to find a little man standing in a mackintosh with its collar turned up and his trilby pulled down over his face. Probably talking fast out of the corner of his mouth, he told Shack that he was a scout and that his boss, Bill Murray, the Chairman of Sunderland football club, was parked just round the corner, out of sight. Clubs were not supposed to talk to players in those days, only to other clubs, Shack, always mischievous, told the scout that he was going out with his wife Marjorie but would be back later. After they'd returned, the scout reappeared at his door and repeated that the Sunderland chairman was in a car outside. Shack followed him and found the car hidden away from the street lights in the shadows, so as not to be seen. The Sunderland chairman did not beat about the bush: he asked Shack to come to join his club.

And so Shack came to us – that is, to Sunderland, where I hardly missed a home game between the ages of eight and eighteen. He was twenty six years old and played in front of crowds of up to 75,000, more than half the male population of Sunderland. He was loved from the start, and played at Roker Park until the end of his career. He scored 101 goals for Sunderland, but was adored more for his dazzling skill and mischievous humour than the goals.

His international career, however, was less than successful. He was already playing for England only a year after the war finished but he was summarily dropped after three games, and did not play again for six years. It was a period of steep decline in England's performances. Starting as the favourites to win the 1950 world cup, they were beaten in the first round by the USA and were then destroyed by Hungary, 6-3 and 7-1 in 1953. The slump took place under the plodding patrician management of Walter Winterbottom, a stiff pedant. The reasons for the bypassing of Shack were not entirely transparent. His uniquely quick thinking on the pitch had already caused problems with centre forwards who did not know what he was going to do next, especially Trevor Ford at Sunderland and Charlie Wayman at Newcastle United. And he also had a less than respectful attitude to middle class managers. But the main reason is probably that Winterbottom and the selectors did not trust the pyrotechnics and wizardry of Shack.

After being excluded from the World Cup squads in 1950 and also in 1954, he was unexpectedly recalled to play the new world champions, West Germany in 1955. It was a pleasing swansong: England won 3-1 and Shack played well, scoring a goal that was described by Stanley Matthews as the best he had ever seen. But he was dropped for the next game.

He never played for England again.

In 1955, when he was still playing for Sunderland Shack published his book (yes, a footballer wrote a book!). The title was "The Clown Prince of Soccer" but the content revealed a serious sense of purpose, and it sold out immediately.

Its most celebrated chapter was a blank page, with a footnote at the bottom that explained that that the author has left this page blank on purpose. The title of the chapter was "What the average football club director knows about football."

But much of it was a serious indictment of the antediluvian rules under which footballers were employed. He described the standard player's contract as "an evil document". It gave the club the right to refuse to release the player after the end of his contact, resulting in at least one very famous player in the north east ending his life in poverty; and it allowed transfers to new clubs without consulting the player.

He also railed against the maximum wage of £17 a week which was little more than an lowly office worker's salary, and he presented the extraordinary statistic that less than half a percent of the cup final takings went to the players. This was £80 less than to the massed bands that played before the game and at half time.

The reviews of the book were positive, although it elicited predictable outrage from some readers. It was regarded as instrumental in the eventual abolition of the maximum wage.

Three years after the book was published, Shack had an ankle operation. He was told he would be a cripple if he continued playing and he retired at 35.

He was not as pure as the driven snow. He admitted in 1996 that he had received an under the counter payment when he was transferred to Sunderland and later used the deal to blackmail the Sunderland Chairman. Shack had not been on good terms with the directors after his book, and when he raised the subject of a testimonial match - which was a common way of giving a player a leaving bonus - he found that they were playing for time. It was only when he resorted to hinting that he might go to the press about the Chairman's own illegal payments to players that the club capitulated. The Times commented that "had the spectators at Roker Park known about the deal they would probably have regarded any inducement as money well spent in return for having Shackleton's skills to entertain them".

But his claim that he was not driven by a desire for money is probably plausible. He just thought the whole system was rotten.

Unlike many footballers he did make provision for his future. Towards the end of his playing career he had already started confectionery, off licence and hairdressing businesses, and he went on to work for the Daily Express as a football journalist for six years and then The People for another twenty years.

He had three children but none became professional sportsmen. They worked as a solicitor, a surveyor and a doctor.

3
The North East after the War

In the year that Len Shackleton signed on for Sunderland, much of the town centre was rubble. It was only three years after the end of the war, and Sunderland had been the seventh most heavily bombed town in England - targeted by the Germans because it had the busiest shipyards in the country. Two particular raids in 1943 had destroyed both the centre and many of the cramped rented houses in the cobbled streets on the outskirts, killing about 250 people. The town bore the scars not only of the blitz but also the recession of the 1930s which had hit the local coal mines as well as the shipbuilding. The Jarrow March of 1936 – to protest against poverty and unemployment in the North East - had begun its journey to London just six miles away.

Most goods were scarce in those years, with food, sweets and clothes still rationed until the 1950s. I did not see bananas until I was four, and despite my mother being a keen cook and a domestic science teacher, spam, baked beans, corned beef and condensed milk loomed large in our diet. About 80% of men smoked, encouraged by Stanley Matthews – rather surprisingly, as he was a teetotal, near vegetarian non-smoker.

There were few cars on the roads and most of them were little black Austin Sevens and Ford Populars, although the owner of the construction company in our village had an ostentatious yellow Vauxhall Cresta. Few houses had telephones; in emergencies we went out to the nearest telephone box with our pockets full of pennies.

In our village - it was three miles away from Roker Park, part dormitory suburb for Sunderland and part pit village – there were throwbacks to poorer times. One that has stayed in my memory was of the men who delivered coal to the dark cellar at the end of our garden - thundering in through a little wooden door opening out into the back lane. It was emptied from sacks by stocky, frightening figures, blackened with coal dust, except for their eyes. They were cruel to the spavined horses that pulled their wagons. Our parents told us that the horses ended up in the butchers' shops in Sunderland, via the knacker's yard, a term I did not understand but did not want to ask about. On other days the silence in the street was broken by the harsh, incomprehensible cries of rag and bone men, knife sharpeners and fish sellers - threatening figures with angry mediaeval faces.

Most of our entertainment came from the radio, in programmes of memorable dullness – including Mrs Dale's Diary, Wilfred Pickles's Have a Go, and John Arlott's leisurely monotonous cricket commentary that was "the sound of the English summer". There was only an hour a day for children until Jet Morgan and Journey into Space arrived in the 1950s.

Glamour was in as short supply as the sweets we bought with our ration books. The newspapers' gossip columns hardly fizzed with excitement, devoting their pages to deferentially respectful stories of royalty, and a middle aged couple from the midlands called Sir Bernard and Lady Docker. They were rich but graceless and plain, and famous mainly for having five Daimlers with seat coverings in crocodile, lizard, zebra and mink. In the absence of home grown celebrities , our newspapers had to look abroad for glamour and developed a long fascination with an exotic "playboy" called Porfirio Rubirosa - a rich polo player from the Dominican Republic who offered a glimpse of an unknown world of free living and promiscuity. Immaculately dressed in white dinner jackets and correspondent shoes, his conquests and five marriages included Zsa Zsa Gabor and Barbara Hutton, the richest woman in the world. I recall being bemused by stories in the newspapers my parents left lying around by references to his "prodigious appetite for women". The gossip columns suggested he might have had mixed blood. "Is the world's greatest lover a Negro?" ran one headline, above a picture of Rubirosa's handsome light-skinned and aristocratic European features. The suspicion will have arisen because a man so addicted to untold pleasures inaccessible to the British reader could hardly have been a white man. He was believed to have had a male member of astounding size, inspiring Parisian waiters to name their gigantic pepper mills "Rubirosas". He also raced cars and fittingly – and perhaps deservedly in the opinion of the gossip column readers - died in a car crash. We at home had nothing like him. There were no Poshes and Becks in those grey days. Our footballers lived in digs and could not afford cars.

We did, however have the cinema, and once a fortnight we would see yet another film of cowboys and Indians, often preceded by tunes played by a resident organist.

A special treat once or twice a year was a visit to the Sunderland Empire to see a music hall show with conjurers, dancing girls, clowns and magicians. It had a grand staircase which only the well-off had been allowed to use before the war. There had been a separate entrance for the working people. But the distinction was abandoned after the war.

* * *

But despite the post-war austerity, it was in many ways a good time. Life was quiet, simple, decent and orderly. The privations of the war were over and the men had returned home to their hobbies of gardening, carpentry and reading. In the evenings they went to the pub, and the young men went along with their elders. The word "teenager" did not yet exist. Nor did "rock n' roll" and as the world waited for its invention the radio played relentlessly cheerful records by Doris Day, Alma Cogan, Billy Cotton and Winifred Atwell for my mother sing along to as she washed by hand, scrubbed on her draining board, and dried the clothes in mangles. Much effort was devoted to making do and mending, darning of socks, sewing, knitting and needlework, and a Singer sewing machine was a prized possession. In the evenings there were Beetle drives in church halls, letter writing and visits to the library. A social survey of the time quoted a lady interviewee: 'What could be better than a comfortable old armchair, a cosy little fire and a good book?'

Adults played little sport. I recall being amazed to find when there were parents' races at school sports day that a few of them could run.

Hooliganism was rare and respect for adults was, even twelve years later, widespread. When I was eighteen noisy teenagers on the last bus home after a night in the pub could be silenced by an adult's voice from the back seat, "Quite enough of that, boys."

* * *

By far the main leisure interest in Britain in these quiet orderly times was football. The year that Shack arrived at Sunderland was the peak year for Football League attendance, with 41 million spectators. By 1953 it had fallen to 36 million. Support was greatest of all in the North East with its three top teams – Sunderland, Newcastle United and Middlesbrough.

The big gates – reaching a post-war record for Sunderland of 68,000[3] at their 1950 home match against Newcastle United - were possible because most of the supporters stood. The move to compulsory all-seater grounds came only forty years later when the Hillsborough deaths led to the Football Spectators Act. The capacity of Sunderland's new all-seater ground, the Stadium of Light, built in 1997, is only 49,000.

In the years that I watched Shack, however, I sat in the seats only once, at a Christmas Day Match against Newcastle in

---

[3] The pre-war record at Sunderland was 75,118, at an FA Cup match against Derby in 1933.

1951. I went with my uncle and it was a great treat, but I remember enjoying it less than I had expected. I had asthma that day, and Sunderland lost 1-0, but I think the real reason was that I missed the warmth and intimacy of the bodies on the terraces as they heaved and jostled for a better view as Sunderland's fortunes ebbed and flowed.

The Roker Roar, which could be overwhelming and inspiring when the team was playing well, was by far the greatest expression of local pride in the North East. We were the only club never to have been relegated from the First Division, and our sense of identity was intensified by rivalry with Newcastle United, twelve miles away.

The play was tough, with shoulder charges and hard tackling, but not dirty.

At first sight the crowds appeared almost entirely working class. The clothes, still functional and drab in the post-war years, seemed a giveaway: most of the crowd dressed in limply hanging raincoats and caps and smoked at half time, mainly Woodbines, the working man's cigarette. But a survey of a typical English club in the late 1940s showed a different picture: it concluded that almost 30% of the supporters were middle class[4]. This was consistent with the facts that over thirty per cent of state-educated children went to grammar schools immediately after the war, and that rugby, the game favoured by the middle classes, and also by grammar school headmasters with social aspirations, was not as popular in the North East. The boys I remember best from those atmospheric afternoons at Roker Park were Bryan, a tall boy with greatly admired hair who went on to be the chairman of some of England's top companies; Ragna, a tiny extravert with a jutting jaw who became a teacher; Billy, my brother, who is now an expert in health services; Geoffrey, a posh boy in a hound's-tooth sports jacket; and Dave Gregson who was a labour party supporter in his early teens and religious. All except one went to a direct grant grammar school.

---

[4] Source: Family Britain by David Kynaston (2009). The survey was carried out in Derby.

There was much vigorous, often splenetic, swearing around us but the atmosphere was unthreatening, and I do not recall 'f' or 'c' words at Roker Park.

There were, however, very few grammar school boys in the top teams, because they would have expected to earn incomes well over the footballers' maximum wage in middle class professions.

Meanwhile, the footballers themselves were kept anchored in the working class by the maximum wage. Not many of them had cars. They often took the bus to games, rented houses owned by the clubs and were deferential to club directors. A typical case was that of Stewart Mitchell, the goalkeeper for Newcastle United in their golden period when they won the FA Cup three times. He lived with internationals like George Eastham in a series of digs where they were served their evening meal by the landlady, and he had no car for his first five years at the club, travelling by public transport until he proudly bought himself a Morris 1000. Until then the only one of the team's stars to have a car was Frank Brennan who, Mitchell said, "had a wee white van ... after all he was a greater star than me ... Brennan was the only guy with wheels. Wor Jackie (Milburn) and Mitch (the Scottish international, Bobby Mitchell), two of the biggest superstars, used to come to the ground in the back of a bus with the supporters. Footballers in the early 1950s - when United were kings - were very much 'of the fans'. They shared public travel, family shops, and places of entertainment."

Even the very top players – such as Tom Finney and Jackie Milburn - did not set out to conquer the world. They were local boys who stayed with their home clubs throughout their playing days, and were accused of being traitors if they ever suggested that they might leave.

It was only in 1963 when George Best started at Manchester United (just two years after the abolition of the maximum wage) that the glamorous celebrity footballer was born.

4

Roker Park: A Saturday Afternoon in the 1950s

I remember it like this….

We were one down at half time. The grown-ups were rolling cigarettes and conversation around the ground was subdued. We had hardly noticed that we had been getting cold in the excitement of the first half and now we stamped our feet and clapped our gloves together to warm ourselves. On the coldest days we fought our way out to buy a plastic cup of hot Bovril. Its smell was the smell of Roker Park.

Above us the sky seemed low, laden with rain, intimate like a large grey tent over our heads as we stood pressed together in the dense crowd. The sun must have broken through on some Saturdays but when it did I recall it being silvery, watery and flat, casting no shadows on the pitch. From high up on the terraces came the bleak cries of seagulls perched on the flag poles, silhouetted against the pearly sky. From time to time they flew off, soaring, banking, wheeling and swooping before settling back on their perches. In the distance foghorns could be heard in the mouth of the River Wear, where the tugs laboured as they dragged their barges against the tide in the oily water, with their freight of steel for the shipyards. Sunderland after the war was still one of the world's great shipbuilding towns and the grey cranes filled the skyline.

The Sunderland of my memory was unremittingly grey in those days after the war. The grey debris from the blitz still lay in the town centre. We had grey school informs, grey school socks and grey ration books for our sweets, and at the cinema we saw grey newsreels - of the liberation of Auschwitz (the pictures gave me nightmares for years), of Roger Bannister running the four minute mile, of the Queen's coronation and of the amateur cup final between Corinthian Casuals and Bishop Auckland on a muddy foggy pitch. On the outskirts of our mining village the echoing grey gasometre with its sour pungent smell of coal gas towered up behind the soot-grimed railway station.

These memories are of course filtered through photographs that were always in black and white - in that monochrome interlude between the nostalgia bathed sepia prints of an earlier age and the colour prints of our bright modern world. Not only that: in the depression of the Thirties it became fashionable to add a further filter of graininess; the best photographs seemed to have been taken through grimy windows streaked with soot and rain. And then when printed in newspapers they were made bleaker by being converted into the grey half-tone dots on which even the better papers depended at the time. So although it is doubtful that sunshine was in shorter supply in the 1950s than today, memories surface partly in the photographic style of the day, as if recorded through a 25 shilling plastic Brownie camera and then printed in the Sunderland Echo.

But no matter; black and white and grey would have been all that was needed, as there was little colour to capture in the drab post-war raincoats packed into the stadium on those afternoons. There were not many lasses there in the 1950s, although the presence of just a few somehow warmed the chill of a February afternoon, especially when they turned out to know more about football than we did. Beneath the men's raincoats there would have been a grey pullover or a black suit, which on Sundays was obligatory. And the colours of the flat caps and mufflers came close to camouflage shades. The man in the crowd gave little thought to his clothes in those years after the war: they were to keep you warm and dry, and you wore what everyone else wore. Young people were still to wear the same styles as their fathers for another few years.

In fact, looking back it seems that the men in the crowd were actually a different shape, square and solid, broad of beam and baggy of trouser, in the last years before teenage fashion was invented. They came into the world as fully formed adults on the evening that they were called from their mothers' sides in the kitchen to join the men in the front room and later to take their first beers at the pub. The men they joined in the pub were men who had endured war in foreign countries for six years and had lived through the recession before that; men who had, and respected, authority and gave and followed orders. They knew what Scott Fitzgerald, who had been too young to fight in the First World War, regretted he would never know: whether they would be brave under fire. Above all, they looked old.

Even our heroes, the Sunderland footballers, looked old. With their nicotined fingers, lined faces and eyes close together, they looked like their parents by the time they were twenty five. And it was not a matter of poverty or hard times. The wealthier sportsmen, gentlemen cricketers such as Colin Cowdrey and Godfrey Evans, were plump and sleek and could have been mistaken for their fathers at a distance.

* * *

But for us there was glamour at Roker Park, where rainy Saturday afternoons were illuminated by visits from prestigious teams from ineffably romantic towns in the north west - Preston, Blackpool, Bolton and Burnley. What joy it would have been to have lived there and seen Tom Finney, Stanley Matthews, Nat Lofthouse and Jimmy McIlroy week after week. Our respect for these teams was equalled only by our contempt for the teams from London, the city of soft southerners, Flash Harrys and jockey-sized homo jokiens who lived on their wits rather than sweat like real men. We did not call our superiors guv, like the London salesmen, servants, butlers, bell hops and spivs who sold what we produced. We were taught early by the older kids to shout, "They're wearing pink pants underneath their shorts."

We had other reasons to be proud. Apart from having Shack, the greatest footballer of them all, our history was studded with stars such as Charlie Buchan and Raich Carter. And by the 1950s we had, as the "Bank of England club", spent more than any other team in the country to attract good players.

This 'team of all talents' gave us an identity. We in the north east were not quite a separate country like Scotland, but there was something of an independent Baltic city state about us. Not that we knew what that meant, but what we did know was that we were almost 300 miles away from London and the south, where the BBC was based and broadcast the news in their strangulated Oxbridge accents. It was also where the England selectors lived and favoured their local players. Apart from overlooking Shack they ignored the Newcastle United centre forward Jackie Milburn, almost certainly the best in the country.

We were also, as the team of all talents, able to attract the best teams in the world, such as Moscow Dynamo who came to Roker Park in 1955 to play under the new floodlights, with their legendary goalkeeper, the 'Black Spider', Lev Yashin. He dressed from head to toe in black (in common with other 1950s stars like Richard Boone who played Paladin in "Have Gun will Travel" and Johnny Cash)

This was the time when football chants were just starting up, and perhaps the most memorable of the era was the refrain:

> Aye, aye, aye, aye,
> Our goalkeeper's better than Yashin
> And (our striker) is better than Eusebio
> And (your team) is in for a thrashing

It would have been good to have been able to have sung it that night under the new floodlights in Sunderland, but it was too early, as Eusebio, Portugal's Black Panther, was only thirteen at the time.

Sunderland had another reason for local pride: that we were not Newcastle United. To us, there was something rotten in the club over the Tyne, with its endless internecine fighting amongst the directors. And their Scots were dourer than ours. In particular, they had a flint hard enforcer of a half back in Jimmy Scoular, the dirtiest player in the league. We, in contrast, had congenial Ken Chisholm, a garrulous ex-RAF officer from Glasgow and Willie Fraser a quiet solid goalkeeper from Lanarkshire. Then we came to hate Newcastle even more when they won the FA Cup three times in the 1950s, while we did not win it once.

The loyalty of a Sunderland supporter was unconditional – and that included mine, regardless of how it had started at the age of seven after choir practice. In 'Fever Pitch' Nick Hornby observed that marriages were much more fickle than loyalty to your football team: that you would hardly catch an Arsenal fan slipping off for a bit of extra marital slap and tickle at Spurs when thing were going badly. The idea of ditching Sunderland in a bad season and transferring our loyalties to Newcastle would have been unthinkable.

When Charlie Hurley, Sunderland's greatest centre half, came to dig up the centre circle at Roker Park to transfer it to the new Stadium of Light in 1997 it was found that several players had their ashes scattered there. In fact so many supporters had wanted to do the same that it had started to spoil the grass and the club had to call a halt to the practice.

* * *

Sunderland in the 1950s, however, was not without its problems, and most of them were at centre forward.

After the record-breaking signing, Trevor Ford, refused to play with Shack there was a continuing but vain quest to find a replacement. The list of Ford's successors included "Cannonball" Charlie Fleming, a lugubrious Scot with a domed head who looked like a Latin teacher; a misery from Middlesbrough called Brian Clough; and Ted Purdon, a handsome blond South African of legendary power.

All except Clough were flops, with Ted Purdon, the South African "wildebeest", who started wonderfully, the worst of all. Towards the end of his stay, on a dreary February afternoon, with the score at 1-1 and fifteen minutes to go, he was passed the ball just a few feet in front of the goal where I was standing down near the front of the Roker end. I rose on to tip toe to make sure I saw it, with the beginnings of that incomparable joy of a lucky win late in the game. Predictably, he turned and hoofed it six feet over the bar. There was a muffled groan, and then three long, long seconds of silence. It was ended by a heavy Sunderland accent, just behind me, more in sorrow than in anger.

"Wey, you shovel footed bugger."

It was a typical finish by Purdy. The game once again was ending in disappointment. Hopes of a late winner glimmered faintly for a few more minutes. But then the final whistle blew.

Ten minutes later, having to use the toilet before going home, I squeezed in to see the backs of thirty drab raincoats in a row, facing the wall, heads down as if waiting to be shot. Hunched over an overflowing trench, they shuffled, shook their heads and muttered and spluttered ... "bloody useless", "hopeless buggers", "bloody great puddin' (a reference to Ted Purdon)", "bloody Ray Daniels", "call themselves footballers?" Their default expression was one of the deepest misery. All their disappointments with life were channelled into their rage against the inexcusable squandering of one easy goal. They were in their element, living – even if not loving - every minute of it.

But streaming out of the ground the crowd came alive again. After all it had been a draw, not a loss, and in these days a draw gave half, not one third, of the points of a win. Dissecting the game as they walked home there was a spring in their step; there was a wonderful gallows humour and great knowledge of the game. These were men of few words – god forbid that they should ever talk about emotions - except when it came to football.

Not that Sunderland's record was particularly poor during the nine years that Shack played for them. Their average position was ninth and in some seasons they were at the top for a few weeks, although they never ended the season better than third in 1949 and fourth in 1954. It was less stressful being in the middle or lower down, with none of the pressure to win the next game to keep the challenge up. In the film Clockwise John Cleese was later to sum up how we felt: "It's not the despair that I can't handle: it's the hope, the bloody hope."

Then home to tinned spaghetti on toast in front of the fire. And later, especially after a victory, it was exhilarating to see the result confirmed and printed in the Sunderland Echo. It was coloured pink on Saturdays, when its front page was decorated by a cartoon of a smiling football when we won; a sad football when we lost; and a neutral football when we drew. The first three pages were dedicated to a blow by blow description of the game, printed forty five minutes after we left the ground. Sometimes we ran to the shops to get the paper and read about what we'd already seen before the spaghetti.

The other ritual was listening to the results on the radio at 5pm, with the rising and falling inflection of the announcer's voice betraying the result to listeners before the last score was given:

SUNDERLAND 2 (with a questioning inflection)
Newcastle   1 (with a falling cadence)

Arsenal   0 (with the same questioning inflection)
LEEDS   2 (with rising inflection)

LIVERPOOL 3 (with the same questioning inflection)
EVERTON   3 (with a hint of surprise)

We never tired of intoning the results with the wrong inflection.

* * *

Even at our grandmother's the next day, football eventually took over. Those Sunday afternoons always followed the same pattern. First, board games - Snakes and Ladders, Tiddly Winks and Ludo - were brought out from the storage cupboard for my brother and I. Next, there were picture books of Victorian heroes like General Gordon and Florence Nightingale, read under pools of light thrown on to the floor from the tasselled lamps. But the favourites were the football annuals with pictures of our heroes, their flushed faces and the green turf they played on, all over-coloured like Indian film posters. My brother, who is two years younger, was lukewarm about the annuals at first, but slowly succumbed to our north east religion.

Best of all, we reorganised our cigarette cards. The precious cards were free gifts in our parents' cigarette packets. They were beautifully clear black and white photos of living heroes and legends of the football league. Under the photos were summaries of previous clubs, goals scored, international appearances and, just occasionally, a fascinating personal detail. Nat Lofthouse, the brylcreemed England centre forward, used to train with a carpet slipper on his strong right foot to force him to improve his weaker left foot shot; and when his kneecap was broken it was replaced with an artificial cap made of steel. So the cards told us. They were magic to us.

5
Just How Good Was He?

Just how good was Shack? Sadly, there are only a few seconds of film of him playing in existence. So we must rely on the memories - reliable or otherwise - of those now aged over seventy. And as one of the crowd at Roker Park from about 1950 until he retired in 1957 I thought that he was unrivalled. If I arrived at the ground and found that he was not on the team sheet the afternoon was spoiled. But you, reader, will not want to take the word of a star struck teenager who was only fourteen years old when Shack retired. So let's look at what the football greats of the time thought.

The player generally regarded as the greatest of the era was *Stanley Matthews*, the first winner of the European Footballer of the Year award and the only player to have been knighted while still playing. In 2000, looking back, Matthews said:

> "Len Shackleton was unpredictable, brilliantly inconsistent, flamboyant, radical and mischievous; in short, he possessed all the attributes of a footballing genius which he undoubtedly was. But such a character did not go down well with the blazer brigade who ran English football and had such an important say in the selection of the English team ...
>
> For long periods in a match Len could be quiet, contributing little, but the two or three minutes when he turned on and did something unpredictable would be the moments of the game that provided the supporters with a golden moment to cherish forever. As one supporter once told me, "two minutes of Shack's genius is worth the price of the admission alone"
>
> His talents were extravagant in the extreme, he was inordinately clever and, despite playing to the crowd, I never saw him being selfish to team-mates... For all his

individuality he did buckle down to team play when the mood took him... However in the latter stages of a match when it was evident that the game was won or lost ... he wold proceed to amuse himself and the crowd..."

(From The Way it Was by Stanley Matthews, Headline Book Publishing, 2001)

Jimmy Greaves, the highest goal scorer in English top division football (357 goals) wrote:

"He was the most gifted player of his generation, able to make the ball almost sit up and talk ... My favourite footballer when I was a kid in short trousers ....(but) his extraordinary talent was rewarded with just five England caps. The establishment was terrified of his individualism and showmanship" (Jimmy Greaves, writing in Football's Great Heroes and Entertainers, Hodder and Stoughton, 2007)

Jackie Milburn, Newcastle United and England centre forward, who played with Shackleton from 1946 to 1948:

"Shack was unbelievable. If he had had the guts or the will to want to do well instead of joking and carrying on, he was untouchable as a footballer... He was absolutely tops in ball control. He was doing these things all the time in training, making mugs of goalkeepers. I've seen Jack Fairbrother dive at his feet in training, and Shack would just let him come, then ease the ball away. The ball was only inches away from Jack's finger. He was wild eyed. He would have killed him ...

But ... it was sheer entertainment with Shack. He admitted later that he had no interest in winning. He just wanted to feel that he'd entertained the public. He was unbelievable - but hopeless. Joe Harvey told George Martin we'll never win anything with Shackleton in the team. We've got to get rid of him.

I've got nothing against Len. He was a smashing fellow, but he had no interest other than entertaining the crowd. He would rather beat three men than lay on a winning goals."

Quoted in book by Mike Kirkup (Jackie Milburn in Black and White, Stanley Paul 1990)

Trevor Ford, the centre forward at Sunderland, was Shackleton's great rival - even his arch enemy. He had reservations about him, but confirmed his unusual talent:

"Shackleton is amongst the immortals as a ball player. His dazzling dribbles, his weaving and bobbing with the ball at his feet, is a heartbreak to opponents and a joy to watch, but what a pity his clowning has been allowed to nullify much of the coordination of the forward line ... Twenty one other players on the field were transfixed as Shack did tricks with the ball the like of which I had never seen before. The crowd loved it ...

But where did it get us? Precisely nowhere... Shackleton is described in official handbooks as a slightly erratic **genius** of inside forwards, and is probably the **greatest ball player in British football.** But some inborn desire to turn every game unto a music-hall comedy has earned him the tag "clown prince of soccer".

Another Roker Park nickname, in my opinion more allied to the truth because it is based on the heartbreaks, frustration and human suffering of a string of players. was the 'centre forward's graveyard.' Since the war more centre forwards have bit the dust playing for Sunderland than any club I know... Sunderland had started the 1948-9 season with their new inside right signing from Newcastle and straight away his dazzling dribbles and individual ball jugglery became the hub of nearly every attacking move.

But from those moments on Centre forwards wore a worried look …. Here was a style of inside forward play completely foreign to them."

("I lead the Attack", by Trevor Ford, Stanley Paul, 1957)

Tom Finney was, like the others quoted, another unassailable of the era. He played 76 times for England, and Bill Shankly called him "the greatest player ever to play the game". Finney dismissed the claim that Shackleton was too difficult to play with:

> "I always found him very simple to play with. I just felt he was a very skilful player and great to play with."

Billy Bingham, the Irish international and later manager, and an excellent dribbler himself (except when the pitch was muddy in mid-winter) was perhaps in the best position of all to assess him, having played alongside Shack in Sunderland's forward line for seven years. He said:

> "He was a genius, a master of ball control, the most wonderful dribbler I have ever seen – and that includes Stanley Matthews. Naturally gifted with agility, balance, and length of foot (I think he took a size ten and a half boot) he nevertheless worked at his game with an intensity that might have surprised those who sometimes accused him of shirking some of his inside forward duties."

But Bingham also criticised his friend for his inability, or refusal, to play with Trevor Ford:

> "The situation between Shackleton and Ford had never been a happy one … They appeared to dislike each other off the field and never seemed to strike up an understanding on it. … Each blamed the other for this state of affairs and I suppose there were faults on both sides… Trevor claimed that Shack wouldn't play to him … Considering what a great footballer he was, Shack should

have been able to give any centre forward a reasonable service."

His obituaries in 2000 were unanimous on his skills:

- The Times called him a "supremely gifted ball player ... (with) matchless wizardry on the field."
- The Guardian called him "a perennial maverick and an enormously gifted inside-forward."
- The Daily Telegraph called him "an inside forward of dazzling skill."

So maybe my assessment of Shack, from the perspective of a seven to fourteen year old, was accurate after all.

Where would he rank in the pantheon of football greats – relative to, say, Messi, Ronaldo, Maradona, Cruyff, Cantona, Best, Pele, Garrincha, Puscas, Eusebio, Stanley Matthews, Tom Finney, Wilf Mannion or Raich Carter?

It is a not a question worth tackling, because the criteria for comparing them could be so different. Is our ideal football the magical ball control and the dribbling skills of the Brazilians of the 1960s; or the fluid elegant carousel team movement of Dutch 'total football' with the balletic Johann Cruyff in the 1970s; or the tic-tac precision of the Spain and Barcelona teams with their hypnotic close passing in recent years; or the direct power and fitness of the Germans in 2014. Or is it the speed, muscularity and battling will to win of the English teams that dominated the Champions League just a few years ago?

Even if we could agree on a set of criteria on which to compare them, Shack would not be subject to the same set. Alone amongst the contenders, he deployed his gifts for a different aim – not so much to win matches as to entertain the crowd. And it has to be conceded that he was sometimes lazy.

His obituary in The Times in 2000, however, concluded that "in the memories of the supporters that paid to watch him he was the greatest player of the generation that included Wilf Mannion, Stanley Matthews and Raich Carter".

6
His Three Clubs

Shack's first six years as a professional footballer were with Bradford Park Avenue, a club that eventually went into liquidation in 1974[5]. It was not the best place for a player of his ability to start, but the options available for any footballer in 1940 were limited.

They were limited because normal football was suspended at the beginning of the Second World War (when Shack was seventeen years old). Football grounds were used as military bases, travel to away games was limited to 50 miles, the nationwide divisions of the Football League were replaced by regional leagues (the North Regional League and the South Regional League) and the gates were limited to 8,000 and later 15, 000 in the interests of public safety.

Many professional footballers had their careers ruined by losing six of their best years, with almost 800 joining in the war effort, and others joining the Territorial Army.

The involvement of the top players in the war varied. Tom Finney fought in Egypt and Italy, and Wilf Mannion fought in France and Italy, while Stanley Matthews served in the Royal Air Force. But Matthews, like many top footballers, was stationed in England and was allowed to play in friendly games. Others served in 'reserved occupations', i.e. jobs necessary for the war effort. The main such occupation was coal mining, with 48,000 men brought in to work as Bevin Boys after the government had probably made a mistake by allowing many of the existing miners to join the armed forces. The Bevin Boys eventually accounted for about one tenth of those conscripted in the war. They included Jackie Milburn, Nat Lofthouse and Shack.

The league eventually returned to the pre-war four divisions, First Division, Second Division and Third division

---

[5] It was reborn in 1987 and now plays in the National League North in a small stadium with a capacity of 3500.

with its north-south split. Bradford Park Avenue had been in the Second Division before the war, played in the Northern Regional League from 1940 to 1946, and emer
ged from the war still in the Second Division, along with Newcastle.

It was against this background that Shack signed on for Bradford in 1940 at the age of 18, and played for them until 1946. He walked several miles to the club to sign on Christmas Day. He was paid one pound and ten shillings (£1.50) a week, but the club manager had to admit that they did not have the money to pay him the standard £10 signing on fee.

During these first years back in Bradford - after he had been discarded by Arsenal - Shack also worked assembling electronic equipment for aircraft during the week. As mentioned, he tried to join Stanley Matthews in the Fleet Air Arm, but his employer refused to release him.

These war arrangements for football were good as well as bad for a young player such as Shack, as he was able to play against old First Division terms such as Liverpool and Manchester United. It gave him more scope to develop his own style than the more results-oriented peacetime game; and Ron Greenwood who played with Shack at Bradford and later became the England manager confirmed that Shack was already the finished article in his later years at Bradford – calling him a larger than life crowd pleaser of extraordinary skill[6].

He played 209 games for Bradford, and scored 171 goals, averaging almost one per game. In fact he exceeded a goal per game in the 1944-45 season.

Towards the end of the war, however, Shack faced a problem. GEC, for whom he was still assembling aircraft radios, had only moved to Bradford to escape the heavy bombing at their main factory at Coventry. But as the bombing was winding down they decided to return to Coventry. Shack did not want to leave Bradford and so declined the offer to move to the midlands. Around the same time he received a letter requiring him to join the army for two years of National Service.

---

[6] http://m.espn.go.com/soccer/story?storyId=1050266&wjb=

But he had an option: there were a lot of pits in Yorkshire and his way out, to avoid losing another critical two years of his football career, was to become a Bevin Boy, working in the mines. He hated every minute of it, and skived shamelessly.

His time at Bradford ended on two rather sour notes. First, a group of supporters started to heckle him because he kept the ball and loved to grandstand rather than passing it straight on. They preferred no-nonsense football. Partly for this reason, he asked for a transfer but was turned down. This was his first experience of the powers of the clubs to hold their staff against their will.

But Shack's own wish to leave Bradford was not the main determinant of whether or not it would happen. It was out of his hands. The deciding factor was the potential profit for his owner, the football club. Shack was now worth a lot of money and when the club eventually found a buyer behind closed doors he *was* transferred – to Newcastle United, without his knowledge, without his involvement in the negotiations and without any financial gain. But he was not upset. Newcastle United was a bigger and better club.

* * *

Shack never really settled at Newcastle, despite a start that could hardly have been better. He scored six goals in his first game, a record. It was against Newport County, another second division team. The final score was 13-0, another record, for the league.

But despite arriving in Newcastle on a high and with the war finished, he was still obliged to work in the local coal mines an alternative to national service. He was fortunate in being able to work alongside his friend Jackie Milburn, but he found the job even worse than in Bradford, especially in the winter of 1946-47 which was one of the coldest on record.

He was also unhappy about some of the training arrangements, in particular when the team was sent up the coast to the isolated windswept village of Seahouses to prepare for matches in Spartan conditions.

Meanwhile, Shack had not been pleased with the standard of housing he had been allocated and went on strike, along with the team's captain, Joe Harvey, who had the same complaint. He was called to the directors' boardroom to present his case and found it heavy going facing the men in suits. It was eventually sorted out when he was given a satisfactory house in the middle class suburb of Gosforth (where, according the local version of the old joke, they drank tea with their little fingers delicately cocked and sex was what they delivered the coal in).

Another source of friction was over the manager's demand that Shack, along with the rest of the team, should go to watch

Charlton Athletic, their opponents in the next round if the FA Cup, over Christmas. Shack had already made plans for Christmas and refused to change them.

Then there was a story that seems hard to believe, but is well documented. It was that just before Newcastle were about to play a top team the manager, George Martin, told Shack, in front of the rest of the team, that this was a really important game and that they had to win it. In fact, he told Shack, if you get a hat-trick you can come off. He did score the hat-trick - within half an hour - and walked off the pitch, to the rage of his manager. There is must be some scepticism about the story, particularly because one version of the story has their opponents winning 4-3 after Shack refused to come back on again. But whether apocryphal or not, it illustrates the way Shack was perceived in his time at Newcastle.

There was also a series of trivial incidents that set Shack further against the club, including friction over a taxi fare from a game to the railway station when he had to rush home to see his son when he was dangerously ill in hospital.

Meanwhile his captain, Joe Harvey, was turning against him. He argued that Shackleton was developing into a crowd entertainer rather than a team footballer and seemed more interested in beating four or five men than passing the ball to a better positioned team-mate. He added that "Newcastle would never win anything with him in the team."

This was not a universally held view. In the opinion of Jackie Milburn, the centre forward and star of the team "Len Shackleton was a master craftsman and thanks to him I got among the goals. I clicked with him because I expected the unorthodox. If he ran one way, I ran the other, and sure enough the ball always found me. On the other hand, Len's quick-witted humour often caused me to laugh outright and lose control of the ball."

Later in his life, he liked to use that humour against Newcastle. Two of his most quoted barbs were:

"I've heard of players selling dummies but Newcastle keep buying them," and

"Newcastle has been unlucky with injuries. The players keep recovering."

He would have made a great TV pundit.

* * *

Less than two years after joining Newcastle he moved twelve miles down the road to Sunderland – who bid more for him than Bolton Wanderers - and found home. "I had joined the best club in football," he wrote. "I had made a move which would give me everything I wanted from soccer – the chance to branch out in business, a house of my own in the best part of town, generous and considerate treatment from my employers and the opportunity to find favour with those hard to please gentlemen of the Football Association, the English selectors."

He was not alone in his views. Trevor Ford was even more effusive about being at Sunderland. He "found the officials and playing staff grand people to work with ... When we went to London for an away game we were always sure of a taxi to the West End and the best seats at the theatre, and during the journey back to Sunderland every player that wanted them could have a packet of cigarettes (!). Yes, Sunderland, like Aston Villa, didn't frown on players who liked a smoke. If ever a player felt he was wanted it was at Sunderland ... There was no dashing away... When the practice session was over Sunderland had a wonderful gymnasium, equipped to the last detail. And as far as most players were concerned that last detail was a billiards table. It was just as true and smooth running as most things were at Roker... What a wonderful set of lads they were."

And Billy Bingham felt the same. "I don't think that one member of what the press called 'this bunch of prima donnas' ever thought Sunderland was not a great club to be with", he wrote, continuing "the directors and officials also thought it was a great club and they spared no effort to make sure the players thought it was too. ... Most of the stars were found good part-time jobs and some of them are still today benefitting, directly or indirectly, from this attention to their welfare (Bingham finished an apprenticeship as an electrician that he had earlier started in Belfast in one of the Sunderland shipyards). We lived like lords to varying degrees. There were free lunches every day at the best restaurants in town and free passes to the cinemas.... On away trips there was special training at spas ... The end of the season brought a trip to romantic places abroad, from Israel to North America.... For all this we chiefly owed thanks to our Chairman, Mr E W Ditchburn ... (and) the Manager, Bill Murray... His biggest assets were undoubtedly his tact and diplomacy: he had an unusual knack for smoothing over temporary upsets and differences ..."

It was not his own club that Shack was to target in his withering attack on the football establishment.

7

Football and Social Class

There is a photograph, taken in 1946, showing four men congratulating each other. Three of them are businessmen. They are wearing drab post-war raincoats, three piece suits, club ties and trilby hats - except for their chairman who is wearing a bowler hat and a pince-nez. They would probably have been carrying gold watches on chains in their waistcoat pockets and they may or may not have been freemasons. They are looking very pleased with themselves, because as directors of Newcastle United football club they have just bought the best and most expensive player in English football.

The fourth man, dressed in an ill-fitting suit and hatless, with a short back and sides - maybe he was advised to have it for his first day - is Len Shackleton. Shack had just been sold by Bradford to Newcastle, in a transaction in which he had not participated. He had been called to a hotel early one afternoon by the Bradford Park Avenue chairman, but not told the reason. When he arrived he recognised nobody and sat uneasily in the foyer, feeling ill at ease and out of place. Eventually there was the sound of laughter as a group of prosperous-looking businessmen emerged from closed doors on the floor above and started to come down the stairs. One of them was the Bradford chairman. Reaching the bottom he broke off the conversation, pointed at Shack and said to another of the men, "That's him: he's all yours." The other man was a director of Newcastle United, Stan Seymour.

Shack only found out what he had been sold for later, when he read about it in the newspapers. It was £13,000, which was over thirty times his annual salary and the second highest fee ever paid in England. He, however, received nothing. Although Seymour promised him a small fee under-the-counter payment of £500 equivalent to less than four percent of the transfer fee that night, nothing was written and it was never paid.

These events were not exceptions: as described in Chapters 13 and 17 Danny Blanchflower and Stewart Imlach were treated with same disdain by their 'owners' on the nights of their transfers.

In the photograph Shack had just made the hundred mile journey north to his new home in Newcastle. He would now sign a professional footballer's contract, a contract which, in his book nine years later, he was to denounce as "an evil document". Warming to the subject he went on to argue that the footballer's lot was comparable with that of slaves or serfs - a claim that may have seemed wildly extravagant, but as he laid out the evidence his arguments became more persuasive.

The contract that he - and other footballers - signed could be cancelled at any time by the clubs, but not by the players, who were to spend their careers "dancing on the end of elastic contracts held securely in the grips of their lords and masters. Sometime the elastic is cut, always from above, never from below," wrote Shack. Should the player wish to leave – for understandable, straightforward reasons, for example, because he may not have liked the city or the club - he could ask for a transfer. But the club could, and often did, say no.

Next, Shack would have been issued his professional footballer's booklet which had to be carried at all times. It forbade him to live in a house that had not been approved by the club, to spend weekends away without permission, to wear unapproved clothing for away games, to talk to the newspapers and to dance between Wednesdays and Saturdays.

Then at the end of the player's career, typically around the age of 35 to 40 in those days, he would lose his house and he would face the future without a pension or profession.

How was it possible that these local heroes could have been treated like this? More than half the male population of Sunderland went to Roker Park on some Saturdays. It was the high point of our week, and the talk in pubs and on school buses in the weekdays in between each Saturday was about football.

As with much of English life in the 1940s, the answer lay in class distinction. But it was not the class distinction of upstairs-downstairs. Those upstairs had little interest in football. They played rugby, the game for gentlemen, as I found out when I went to my secondary school, a direct grant grammar school, where it was a subject of simmering discontent that we were obliged to play rugby instead of football because the headmaster's dearest wish was for us to be seen as a public school. He would announce at assembly that one of his criteria for selecting a prefect was the way the boy fell on the ball on the rugby field.

An upper class accent in the crowd was rare at Sunderland or any football ground - one of the few exceptions being A J Ayer, an Old Etonian and professor of philosophy at London and Oxford universities, who was a

Tottenham Hotspur supporter. It was considered an eccentricity, mentioned with simpering amusement when he was introduced on the panel of the radio's weekly intellectual programme, The Brains Trust.

No, football was more "middle stairs-downstairs". It had emerged from the Second World War controlled by businessmen who fought to keep wages low and traded players for profit; and for whom Shack had little respect. And although Shack was intelligent and sharp witted he was a loser in his early skirmishes with his lords and masters.

His first encounter with a football director was at the age of sixteen at Arsenal. There, when ordered in an affected BBC accent to tie the manager's shoelaces Shack, being Shack, could not help blurting out the obvious reply, that he could tie his laces himself - probably precipitating his exit from the club a few months later.

Later, at the age of twenty five he was again a loser, at least temporarily, in a battle with the directors of Newcastle United. It was over a promise by Newcastle to provide him with a semi-detached house similar to the house he had left in Bradford. The club at first failed to honour the promise and when Shack went on strike he was summoned to the board room.

Facing what he called the "the stern looking collection of businessmen turned soccer sages" sitting at the polished mahogany table, surrounded by dark framed pictures of past dignitaries, he nevertheless felt that he could defend himself. But he had not reckoned with the chairman of the board, Alderman McKeag. McKeag was not only a businessman but also a solicitor. He had also been an MP and, deploying his forensic skills as a debater, he pointed out Shack's waywardness "in authentic courtroom fashion". Outwitted, Shack left the room persuaded that it was he rather than the club that was in the wrong. (He wasn't, and to their credit the club relented and gave him the new house soon afterwards.)

Even more imperiously arrogant was the behaviour of Sir Stanley Rous, Secretary of the Football Association, who wrote to the Kenyan football association after they had invited Shack to play in some friendly games and help with some, coaching over a summer. "We are not sure," read the letter, "that we will give permission to Mr Shackleton to act as a coach to your association in view of his attitude to governing bodies."

By that time Shack was winning his battles against the directors. But others were not, including the two other "legendary" super stars of the north east – Jackie Milburn, Newcastle's centre forward, and Wilf Mannion at Middleborough.

"Wor" Jackie Milburn – a friend of Shack's from his Newcastle United days and adored by the public - was humiliated by the directors when he dared to ask for a transfer. Called to the board room to make his case, he had to stand, like Shack, in front of the directors and explain that his wife was suffering from bronchitis and wanted to go south for her health. He was a modest and humble man, too inarticulate to make his case. His masters dismissed him disdainfully from the room. He finished his career at Newcastle and later I saw him selling lawnmowers for a living around the city.

Then down at Middlesbrough Wilf Mannion, their most gifted player and their equivalent of Shack, was offered a transfer to the glamorous Italian club, Juventus. But the Middlesbrough directors would not release him; and later when he insisted on a move to the lesser club of Oldham, they still blocked him. He went on strike, and while he waited for the directors to relent he resorted to selling chicken coops around the town. The "golden boy" of Middlesbrough and England was later to be seen working on building sites. He died in poverty.

Much of this happened behind closed doors, but it was a more public event that exposes how exploitative and mercantile the club directors could be. It happened, again, at Newcastle (our enemy at Sunderland: we always knew there was something rotten over there!).

Newcastle had a popular centre half, the rock-like Frank Brennan, who had been a towering figure in Newcastle's FA Cup wins in 1951 and 1952. Then in 1953, mindful of the need for an income after his retirement, he set up a sports shop near Newcastle's ground at St James's Park. By that time I was going to school in Newcastle and we used to call into his shop just to see the great man, a gentle giant well over six feet. But there was another sports shop in the city, less than a mile away, and it was owned by Newcastle United's most prominent director, Stan Seymour. Reportedly as vindictive as he was bald and fat in his later prosperous years, Seymour set about ruining Brennan.

In the next two years, at the top of his game and only twenty eight years old, Frank had his salary cut from £17 to £8 a week - to support a wife and six children - and he was dropped from the team. Most hurtfully of all, he was not allowed to try for his third medal in the FA Cup final when Newcastle won again in 1955. Meanwhile, the Newcastle footballers, his team-mates, were instructed not to use Brennan's shop. The fans were outraged and called public meetings at City Hall, passing a vote of no confidence in the board. In a passionate speech to the TUC, union militant Jimmy Guthrie said, "I stand here as a representative of the last bonded men in Britain, the professional footballers … We seek your help to smash such a system under which human beings are being bought and sold like cattle. The conditions of the professional footballer's employment are akin to slavery." But the board remained intransigent and as a final insult tried to sell Brennan against his will – effectively to exile the Scotsman - to Plymouth Argyle, the most distant club in the country.

Brennan eventually left to join a minor team in 1956, but in a final snub the Newcastle directors refused him his expected testimonial match at St James Park. He had to arrange it at Roker Park, the home of Newcastle's great rival. Seymour's claim all along was that Brennan's diversification into sports shops would be "a distraction from his football".

In his later years, Frank was never without the two FA Cup medals he did win, keeping them in his trouser pocket at all times.

Shack was eventually to become a keen student of the manners and affectations of his one time overlords, the local dignitaries. It was his observation that important people everywhere like to be seen with other important people, and he had the opportunity to observe the species at close quarters twenty years later on a visit by the North Eastern Sporting Club to Las Vegas.

By this time Shack was a journalist, and another member of the party was his old adversary, William McKeag – who, when he travelled abroad was in the habit of letting local city officials know that he had been an MP, a Lord Mayor and a football club Chairman. When the bigwigs of Las Vegas' city hall heard that another bigwig, albeit from a different world, was in town they decided that they would like to bestow an honour on him. It was to be The Freedom of the City, symbolised by a silver key.

On the night of the ceremony McKeag thought it would be educational for the less eminent members of his party to witness the ceremony, and took them along. There is a photograph of McKeag dressed in a heavy pinstripe suit and wearing a pince-nez on a ribbon. He is standing amongst a group of local politicians and Las Vegas cops chewing gum, staring at him as if he was from a distant planet. Shack can be seen in the background, in a T shirt, smoking a cigar.

When KcKeag stood up to make his speech he seemed to hit a jarringly wrong note and spoke for too long. But what really ruined the night for McKeag was one of the locals sauntering over afterwards and saying to Shack and the others: "Say, guys, how many of you are there in your party?" When told that there were only a few he said "Well, we have lots of these keys here, so you can all have one". And McKeag watched aghast as they were each handed a precious key to the Freedom of the city of Las Vegas.

Shack, however. was no longer downstairs. Although the maximum wage was not abolished until 1961, three years after Shack retired, he had gone on to set up shops, to coach football in Hong Kong and to work for national newspapers as a journalist. And later one of the greatest sources of pride for Shack, the rebel and class warrior, was that his three children had become a doctor, a surveyor and, like McKeag, a lawyer.

8
The Maximum Wage

Wayne Rooney is paid almost £300,000 a week. Obscene, you say; absurd, insulting to the ordinary working man.

A good lawyer, however, could win a case for the defence on at least two grounds. First, the fans fund Rooney's and other footballers' wages, and they do it voluntarily, choosing to spend their money watching football rather than on other things. A second argument, however, would be an appeal for reparations. The case would be strong: it would be that for sixty years the most revered heroes of the mass of ordinary people were kept in relative, sometimes humiliating, penury.

The main instrument of control of professional footballers was the miserly maximum wage, first introduced in 1901 by the Football Association (FA). It was set at £4 a week and enforced until 1960, by which time it had risen by an ungenerous 2.8 per cent a year to £20 a week - the same as my own starting salary around that time as a twenty one year old in a London office.

But why a ceiling on wages for footballers of all people? In 1901 there were no maximum wages for actors, boxers, circus clowns or music hall entertainers, and footballers were already more widely followed that any of them. The reasons take us into England's social history, and they are not edifying.

The maximum wage originated with two bodies, both of which were self-appointed. They were the Football Association and the Football League.

The first, the *Football Association*, was an aloof Victorian group dedicated to the Corinthian ideal of amateurism in sport. They saw sport as a vehicle for developing character on the playing fields of England's public schools - to train the young gentlemen for their responsibilities in governing Britain and the Empire. There was, however, a problem: it was that when the young gentlemen arrived at Cambridge University there was confusion when they found that they were playing to rules that differed by school. The problem was identified by Ebenezer Morley, a solicitor who had set up a football team at Barnes in 1862 and found that the public schoolboys who joined it were having "fevered disputes" about how the game should be played. So in 1863 a group came together at the Freemason's Tavern in London to standardize the rules. The Football Association's first full time secretary was an Old Harrovian and he did his job well. The private schoolboys became rather good at football, being better fed than the players on the professional teams that were just starting up; and when the FA Cup was introduced in 1871 it was contested mainly between amateur teams. In fact the Old Etonians beat Blackburn Rovers to win the FA Cup in 1882.

By the mid-1980s, however, the competition was increasingly dominated by professional teams, and, having completed their task of drawing up the rules for the young gentlemen, the FA took it upon themselves to extend their Corinthian ideal to the football played by working men; and, in particular, to stamp out the professionalism that they deplored. They campaigned against it for twenty years and expelled Preston North End from the FA Cup because they were paying their players. (It was a prejudice that lasted in the ruling bodies in British sport into the 1960s, when the Gentlemen still faced the Players once a year at cricket and the All England Lawn Tennis and Croquet Club outlawed professionals at Wimbledon.) It was only in 1885, after four years of debate, that the FA finally 'permitted' payment of footballers.

Meanwhile, the clubs - that is to say, the employers of the footballers - set up their own organization, the *Football League*, in 1888. Whereas the FA's officials were drawn from the upper echelons of British society the League's were drawn more from the middle classes, many of them local industrialists and businessmen who often owned the clubs. The arguments the owners aired in public to support a maximum wage were that a player was not an individual but part of a team, and that competition had to be kept fair by removing carrots for the best players to move to the best teams. But they probably had more interest in keeping their wage bills low, and exercising their power to keep the best players at their clubs, and under control, by offering them employment in their factories during the week.

Together the Football League and the Football Association had effectively conspired to commit one of the Penny Catechism's 'Four Sins that cry out for Vengeance from Heaven' – the defrauding of labourers of their rightful wages [7]

* * *

Extraordinarily, the wage ceiling was not challenged for another sixty years.

For the first fourteen years of the twentieth century the players came under this strict new regime; and then during the first world war football was put on hold, as most of the players joined the armed forces.

It was when the war finished in 1918 that football really came into its own. After the misery of the trenches the government rewarded the people by building Wembley Stadium. It was designed to hold 127,000, but the first Cup Final attracted a crowd almost three times as great, and mounted police had to be brought in to clear the spectators from the pitch. And other grounds literally collapsed under the weight of spectators. At Chelsea, there were scores of injuries when a roof on to which spectators had climbed collapsed on to the fans.

Ground receipts mushroomed, and even middle-ranking teams reported record takings. For instance, Bradford City finished one season in mid-table and were knocked out of the cup in the second round, but still had gross takings of more than £35,000, and profits after all expenses and taxes had been

---

[7] The other three sins, for interest, are wilful murder, oppression of the poor and sodomy. For those not familiar with the Penny Catechism it is stern little manual used mainly for the instruction of the young in the principles of the Catholic faith, and to warn them that the consequence of failure to follow the true faith, and to renounce the devil "in all his pomp", is Hell. It now costs £1.50.

deducted of £22,000. One reason was that admission fees had been doubled, from 6 (old) pence to one shilling (5p).

For a time the players saw some of the benefit: in 1920 the maximum wage had been £4.50 a week and for the 1920–21 seasons it too was doubled to £9 a week.

But the good times were short-lived. A few years later, with the economic recession looming, many clubs found that they had overreached themselves with expensive ground extensions, and, they claimed, the burden of ever-rising transfer fees. This was disingenuous as the costs of transfers to the buyers were equalled by the incomes to the sellers. But as early as 1922 they decided to cut wages unilaterally. Players' contracts were torn up, and despite the massive attendances, many of them fell on hard times.

Clubs began to hold more and more players on their retain-and-transfer lists without paying them - giving the directors a pool of free labour that they could sell if they could find buyers, even without the players' consent.

By 1939 fewer than 10 per cent of players were in the 'maximum' earning bracket and many had to sign on for the dole to supplement their minimal wages at the over-staffed clubs.

The Second World War came and went but the terms and conditions of the footballers remained the same, or maybe even worse. In 1938, a Jubilee Benevolent Fund had been set up to come to the aid of footballers who had fallen on hard times when they retired, as few of them had much education. The fund quickly built up a kitty before the war started. But by 1947, with the fund up to £47,000, only £1,725 had been paid out. A Football League spokesman claimed that this showed that the players had no real need of assistance.

It was around this time that Shack joined Newcastle United as the most expensive player in England. His transfer fee was £13,000, all of which went to the club. They promised him about 4 per cent of the fee, but then reneged, and over the next year Shack worked in a coal mine to supplement his income.

Increasingly aware that the whole financial set-up was deeply unfair, he became vociferous in crusading against it. His book, written in 1955, contained some telling statistics. He estimated that out of the total gate receipts for a cup final in the early 1950s only *half a per cent* went to the players. The massed bands that played before the kickoff and at half time were paid more, at about £320. There was a bonus of £20 each for the players, but only for the winning team. The losers got nothing.

In fact, a few years earlier, after he had already left Newcastle, Shack had revisited his old club just before the 1951 cup final to explain to them how much the gate money would amount to and the miserly share they would get.

"You want to refuse to go on to the bloody pitch" he said. "Because they're making nearly forty thousand pounds at the gate."

Roger Hutchison's "The Toon: The Complete History of Newcastle United Football Club" recalls that the players took the idea of a boycott seriously but decided that the directors would find others more than happy to play in a Cup Final, even if they were eleven reserves. Rather sadly, the players, including internationals who were household names, were reduced to trying to make a little extra money from the final by putting together a brochure and selling it for two shillings from a trestle table outside their ground in the weeks leading up to the final.

Throughout the 1950s progress on wages remained slow. In 1951 the maximum wage was increased to £14 in 1953; to £17 in 1957; and in 1960 it stood at £20 a week.

By then maximum wages had already been abolished in Scotland, France, Italy and South America, allowing the commercial value of the star players to emerge into the light of day. The Uruguayan inside forward Schiaffino was paid £40 a week when he was transferred to Milan, and also received one third of his £72,000 transfer fee. He had a rent free flat in Milan and was allowed to leave, unlike English players, at the end of his contract. Another player who joined Internazione of Turin received ten per cent of his transfer fee of £30,000.

But in England the controls remained rigidly in place. At the Trades Union Conference of 1955 the representative of the players, Jimmy Guthrie made a speech deploring the way footballers were treated by their clubs. He first attacked ,the rules preventing players from leaving their clubs, describing professional players as "little better than slaves". He went on:

"We have had enough of bondage ... We seek your assistance to unfetter the chains and set us free."

He then turned to the maximum wage, arguing that in 1939 the footballers' £8 a week had been approximately double the average industrial wage, but by the 1950s the gap had narrowed to about 40%.

In the same year Shack attacked the parsimony of the patrician bodies that controlled football in his book. He recalled how he played for England at Hampden Park in front of a gate of 130,000 but was paid only 30 shillings (£1.50) plus a third class rail ticket; how he had to pay his wife's fare; how they had to stand on the way back; and how Walter Winterbottom, the England Team Manager, would not let the captain, Billy Wright, keep his shirt after the game.

His efforts were not in vain. Two years later, the Professional Footballers Association embarked on a campaign for long overdue reforms. The events leading to its eventual success are followed up in the chapters on the end of the maximum wage and the footballers contract.

9
Shack's Nine Years at Sunderland

Argus, the Sunderland Echo's football reporter during the nine years that Shack played at Sunderland, covered the joys and occasional disappointments of watching Shack week by week.

* * *

January 26th, 1948.

The week before Shack joined Sunderland, they were close to bottom of the First Division (the predecessor of the Premier League). They were fearing relegation for the first time in their history. Argus wrote:

> "Never within my memory have I seen what we saw at the final whistle ... fewer than half the number of spectators still in the stands ... It was a visible expression of disgust at the attempt of twenty two professional players trying to produce top-grade football... Sunderland football never (before) sank to the low level of the present day."

February 9th, 1948.

A week after signing Shack, Sunderland were still close to the bottom of the First Division, but, wrote Argus:

> "I was delighted at Shackleton's display of craft and his speed over ten yards on his first appearance in Sunderland colours."

March 1st, 1948.

Four weeks after he joined Sunderland, they were still third from bottom. But Shack had made a difference:

> "That goal of Len Shackleton's was a real beauty and in Sunderland's team he was the outstanding figure... But there are some features of his play which, while showing great individual skill, I can liken to Willie Watson's inside forward play. Shackleton's magnificent football skills open up a defence, and then he hangs on for a few yards, which means that opponents can cover his colleagues. All the same he is a delight to watch ... (although) ... I sometimes wonder whether his colleagues have quite yet fathomed what he intends to do when he gets the ball."

Shack's performances in the last three months of the season saved them from relegation.

Feb 4th 1950

Two years later:

> "I have not changed my view that Len Shackleton is the best player in England today. It may be that certain people who have a big say in the selection of the England team have other ideas, but that won't alter the views of the Sunderland supporters on Shackleton... and his value to Sunderland."

March 4th 1950

> "Some people are already talking of Sunderland as the 1949-50 League Champions. .. Sunderland's play gives a great deal of entertainment and that is proved by the average attendance at Roker Park being over 50,000, and the further fact that on other grounds attendances are above the average when Sunderland pay a visit ... *But I hesitate to think what might happen if ... Sunderland lost Len Shackleton for four or five games* ... All Tommy Wright's grit and persistence at outside right would not make up that loss, for Shackleton is not only the brains of the line – he is the maker of the line, and you can see the consequences when he has, as all players have

> occasionally, an indifferent game. When Shackleton came to Sunderland from Newcastle many people thought the Roker Park directors financially mad to pay £20,050 for the player. He has not only been worth every penny of it, but in my judgment his transfer fee can be written down to nil because of the increased revenue from the gates he has attracted. There is not the slightest doubt he is a box-office attraction on every ground: there is not the slightest doubt, either, that he is a football genius and like a genius he has that trait of doing a thing in a difficult way when it could be done in a simpler way. Len seems suddenly to make up his mind that he is going to do a thing in a certain way and does it - and does it accurately. It is not playing to the gallery: it is simply that kink of the football genius that puts him so far above most of his fellows in the game."

May 6th 1950.

By 1950, Shack's skills were sufficiently recognized abroad for his possible absence from the team to have endangered a tour to Turkey:

> "The Turkish trip has given Mr. Murray many headaches and these were intensified when the FA announced that Watson and Shackleton were wanted for England's B team. But the Turkish authorities put the cat amongst the pigeons by saying "Shackleton for four games or the tour is off.""

April 14th 1951

Sunderland 4 - Everton 0

> "Sunderland, in brilliant form, outplay a shaky Everton side ... It was for Shackleton another really great triumph. He schemed and fought every minute of the game ... Shackleton has rarely been more effective and the Everton defence had no answer to his craft".

April 28th 1951

> "Other important factors (in Sunderland's improved performances) have been the return to form and fitness of Len Shackleton …..Len's injured groin was pronounced fit early in March, but it has taken ten games since then to clear up the more important aspect of the injury – restoration of confidence. …Two "all-in" games against Everton and Stoke City have put Len right on top of the world again."

1953/4 season

The 1952/53 season had been reasonably successful with Sunderland finishing 9th.in the First Division But as relations between Shack and Trevor Ford deteriorated in 1953/4 the team dropped to 18th

March 20th 1954.

In 1954 Shack was not consistently good. By March Sunderland were struggling and Argus wrote:

> "Len Shackleton.. Will he repeat his "rescue act" of 1949? Sunderland could certainly do with him in top form at this stage."

> He went on to argue that the answers to Sunderland's problems were tied up...

> "… very closely with one man ... Len Shackleton ... Sunderland officials have allowed themselves to drift into the position where the play of this unpredictable genius is the key to the performance of the team as a whole. At his best Len is a very good player and it is upon his best play that his form must be judged. (But) over the past few weeks he has been unbelievably bad and the side has been struggling... Is it fair to pin so much responsibility on one player? Shackleton supporters, and they are legion, will be

quick to come to the defence of their favourite... For myself I do not pin the blame entirely on Len. He has a particular style of play, well suited to the team leading by three to four goals with half an hour left for play, but he is not so prominent in a team 2-0 down and only a few minutes to go.

"The indecisive Shackleton is the present-day player. There are occasional flashes of the really fine player that he can be, but nothing nearly as consistent as he was when first arriving in the north east. His first season with Newcastle United was terrific and when he was transferred to Sunderland in 1948 his inspired play was perhaps the greatest single factor in rescuing the club from the dreaded drop into the Second Division ..."

"Whether he can recapture that form is the big doubt that assails Sunderland supporters. Those who look for brightness in their football will tell you that Len's brand of genius cannot be bettered. There are others who will say that Len's lack of strength is one of the great weaknesses in the side. But they would not go to watch the team play if he were not on it."

"I think that the serious minded Shackleton is the one who can make it a winning fight ... He can make the team effective but he can also pull it down to very low levels. In the next game or two he can indicate whether he is prepared to work exclusively to the requirements of the team and club rather than the glory of self-achievement."

December 4th 1954

By 1954/55 Shack was back on form and Sunderland finished 4th.

Shack had just played for England and Argus commented that:

> "Stanley Matthews and Len Shackleton alone looked like the highly skilled players we are accustomed to seeing in the vastly different setting of a League game."

December 18th 1954

Sunderland were in second place in the First Division, and in the game against West Bromwich Albion:

> "Even the Albion crowd applauded Shackleton's skill."

April 30th 1955

> "For seven years the one constant factor in attack has been Len Shackleton ... It was upon his excellent play that he was able to draw from the remainder of the forward line in the early months of the season that led to the high hopes of a successful season ... The sharp decline in his play from the half way stage, however, only showed the extent to which the remainder if the forwards were dependent on him for craft .. The pattern of results in the last four months is a clear enough indication of what Shackleton in indifferent form and frequently absent has meant to the side"

(Shack was probably nursing injuries at this time)

Nov 19th 1955

Sunderland lose 8-2 at Luton Town despite being in fifth place in Division One.

> "Shackleton has never been further out of a game. How he expected results to be achieved for the quality of support he gave his colleagues is difficult to understand."

This was Shack's eighth year with Sunderland and he had been suffering with ankle injuries for three years before this report.

The recurrent injuries forced him to retire at the end of the 1957/58 season, after the doctor told him that if he did not he would be crippled for life. It is presumed that this was the reason for his decision. Another contributory factor, however, might have been his dislike for the new manager who took over from Bill Murray at the beginning of the 1957/58 season. His successor, Alan Brown, was a disciplinarian who did not like untidy dress, long hair and tepid enthusiasm for the running track. Shack called him a 'terrible manager'. He played one game under Brown and then sat out the rest of the 1957-58 season injured before retiring. Brown then went on to resist Shack's request for a benefit match after ten years of outstanding service to the club.

* * *

In the nine years that he played for them:

- Shack was generally acknowledged to have saved Sunderland from their first ever relegation from the First Division when he joined them in 1948; and

- the club remained in the First Division for the next nine years, until Shack retired in 1957, and were relegated at the end of that season.

10

His International Career

Shack played his first game for England Boys at the age of thirteen and his last game for the senior team at the age of thirty three. But in the intervening nineteen years he won only five full caps.

Did he care? This was the player whose manager said towards the end of his career that Shack *cared little for praise or damnation*.

But of course he cared. It is revealing that *both* the first and the last chapters of Shack's book were about his being recalled by England after years of rejection – and, having played well, being dropped and never playing again.

His ascent to international level was as fast as it was possible to be. At eleven years of age he was able, after passing the scholarship exam, to choose where he went to school and he selected a grammar school across town that had the best football team. A tiny football prodigy, he was soon the captain of the team, scoring forty goals in fourteen matches; and at thirteen one of his teachers put him forward to play for the North versus the Midlands schoolboys. Despite being the smallest player on the pitch at 4' 11" he excelled and was selected to play for the England Schoolboys team against Wales. Even at international level he stood out, scoring two goals in a 6-2 victory. He then went on to play for England again when they beat Scotland 4-2 and Northern Ireland 8-3

His football was interrupted by the war, but within a year of its ending he made the full England team in 1946, in a home international against Scotland that was followed by another against Wales. He won his first international cap against Denmark in 1948 when they drew the game 0-0. It was team that included 'legends' such as Stanley Matthews, Tommy Lawton, Jimmy Hagan, Billy Wright and Frank Swift.

But over the next six years he was left out in the wilderness.

The period during which he didn't play saw an alarming decline in the once great English team. It took place under the administration of **Walter Winterbottom** who had been appointed as England's first ever full-time manager in 1946. (The team was still picked by a committee until <u>Alf Ramsey</u> took over as manager in 1963.)

Four years after Winterbottom took over, England played in the World Cup for the first time, in 1950. The immediate reason for their not having played until then was a dispute with FIFA over payments to amateurs, but it was also said that the English football establishment considered their team too good for the rest of the world. They saw themselves as the "Kings of Football", with a post-war record of 23 wins, 4 losses, and 3 draws. They had recently beaten the Italians 4–0 and the Portuguese 10–0 in Lisbon. The Americans, in contrast, had lost their last seven international matches by a combined score of 45–2, including losses to Italy (7–1), Norway (11–0) and Northern Ireland (5–0). The odds were 3–1 against the English winning the Cup, and 500–1 against the USA.

But in the first match of the tournament the USA won 1-0, and England, supposedly the best team in the world, had fallen to a team amongst the lowest ranked in the world.

Worse followed. In 1953 they suffered their first defeat by a foreign team at Wembley, losing 6-3 to a Hungarian team that included Puscas, Czibor and Hidegkuti; and in the return match in **Budapest**, Hungary won 7–1. It was and still is England's worst ever defeat. After the game, centre half Syd Owen is reported to have said "it was like playing men from outer space".

Then in the 1954 World Cup England went out in the quarter finals, and the tournament was won by West Germany, who beat Hungary in the final. Shack was not in the squad.

But this calamitous decline did not undermine the Football Association's support for Winterbottom. The attitudes of the governing bodies in English football had been exemplified just before the war on a tour of Europe. The first game was against Germany in Berlin, and Hitler wanted to use the game as a showcase for Nazi propaganda. Just before kick-off a Football Association official arrived in the English dressing-room, and told them that they had to make the Nazi salute during the playing of the German national anthem. Stanley Matthews later recalled that "the dressing room erupted. There was bedlam. All the England players were livid and totally opposed, myself included. Everyone started shouting at once. Eddie Hapgood, normally a respectful and devoted captain, wagged his finger at the official and told him what he could do with the Nazi salute, which involved putting it where the sun doesn't shine." The FA official left, but returned saying he had an order from the British Ambassador, Sir Neville Henderson, that the players must make the salute, because the political situation between Britain and Germany was now so sensitive it needed "only a spark to set Europe alight". Reluctantly the England team raised their right arms, *except for Stan Cullis who refused, and was subsequently dropped from the squad.*

Winterbottom personified these patrician attitudes. He had had no previous managerial experience in professional football and spoke to the team like a schoolmaster holding a tutorial. His accent was rather upper class (a characteristic shared with other adversaries of Shack, including Arsenal's George Allison and Newcastle United's William McKeag) and this grated with Shack. It was recorded that Winterbottom once told them that he wanted "all you five forwards to run down the field, interpassing the ball, until you come to the goal, where there'll be no goalkeeper. Then put the ball into the net." Shackleton, lying on the ground, looked up: "Which side of the net, Mr Winterbottom?" he asked.

The most frequently quoted reason for Shack's omission from the English team was that given by an unnamed England selector who, when asked "Why is Len Shackleton consistently left out of the England team?", replied: "Because we play at Wembley Stadium, not the London Palladium." This was a good quote. But there were other reasons for Shack's absence. It was the consensus amongst the best players that he was just too clever. Moreover, he was a maverick, believing that the point of football was as much to entertain as to win; others could not think as fast on the pitch; and the selectors did not like Shack's 'agin the government' wit. There was also a belief that northerners have less of a chance of catching the selectors' eyes than teams playing close to London.

Winterbottom, whose approach was pedestrian, found Shack's maverick ways unworkable. "Len was the type of person who could take the stage himself and wanted to more often than not ...He'd trick a player and then he'd turn round and beat him again - there's no need to do it! And he would try fancy tricks when a good straight pass was on." Winterbottom would tell of his unsuccessful attempts to 'tame' Shack for the England set up – "If only Len would come half-way to meet the needs of the team there wouldn't be many to touch him." He did, however, acknowledge that "it was clever and the crowd loved it".

Against this background, and having missed the World Cup, Shack was surprised to be recalled to play West Germany, the new world champions, in 1954. He claims in his book that although he regarded it as a great honour; he was by this time disenchanted with the idea of ever playing for his country again. But two considerations changed his mind. First, he was attracted and excited by the idea of playing the world champions, regretting his not having been involved in the World Cup; and, secondly, he thought it would give a kick start for a new hairdressers' shop he was opening! But there was an initial hurdle. Before playing West Germany he had to play in a routine game against Wales, and in order not to jeopardise his prospects for the German game, he had to obey orders - avoiding dribbling, and passing the ball immediately. A selector congratulated him on playing just how they wanted. Shack was horrified. And so was a sports journalist who asked him why he had played that way, "passing the ball as if it were red hot". Shack replied that he should wait until the game against Germany. "I might show you something that day and explain about the Welsh game."

The instructions for the West German match were the same, and Shack obediently played a conventional passing game for half an hour. But then he switched - back to his normal game, dribbling and weaving through the German defence. Half way through the second half he almost scored what Stanley Matthews described as "what would have been the greatest goal of all time." Matthews recalled: "He came over to the right and I slipped the ball to him and ran on for the expected through pass. It never came. Instead he swivelled and ran right through the German defence. He even beat the goalkeeper but, unluckily, the ball ran out of play. The rest of us could only stand and marvel at the cheek of him."

But then he did score a goal, and Stanley Matthews described it - Shack's last goal in his last game for England - as the finest he ever saw in international football. "He took a pass from me at the half way line, cut inside, went through the German defence and lobbed the ball cleanly over the keeper." (The Times, obituary for Shackleton, 2000.)

It was not quite the victory it seemed. The World Champions had been weakened by an outbreak of jaundice, while England had ironically been strengthened by the withdrawal of several of the more plodding regulars, resulting in the selection of a brilliant side of ball players, including Stanley Matthews and Tom Finney as well as Shack. They played some exciting football, and Shack's goal was the highlight.

Shack himself called it the most memorable goal of his career. He said that "it is not easy to explain, but I felt a keen satisfaction ... because I had decided exactly how to go about scoring it before the chance presented itself. Anticipation and fulfilment."

He was dropped for the next game. He speculated that it might have been because he broke the rules by talking to a Swiss journalist who asked him why Germany had lost the game. Shack replied that the Germans were using the square ball and it can be painful when you head it. Also, the selectors remembered that he had asked for a first-class rail ticket from Sunderland, instead of the third-class ticket prescribed by the

Football Association. But it might have just been the same old story: Jimmy Greaves, the highest ever goal scorer in English top division football, believed that the England selectors remained "suspicious of such an outrageous talent", and "terrified of his individualism and showmanship".

It was to be Shackleton's final England appearance. In 1955, he published his book, "The Clown Prince of Soccer" in which he said that "there are so many things wrong with British international football and so few things right that I can quite honestly state I have no desire to be capped again."

He was unrepentant. An obituary quoted him saying later:

"I am tired of Britain being the laughing stock of world football. I want to see the country on top again. I do not take back a single word."

11
The Secrets of His Success

The secret of Shack's success at football was straightforward: he was preternaturally talented at all ball games – or at least those involving a moving ball.

At cricket, which was by far the main summer game in England in those days, he played for two counties, Durham and Northumberland. They were both minor counties at the time, but it was said that he could have played first class cricket - like his Sunderland team mate Willie Watson and Denis Compton, the England winger. He was the resident professional for seven years for a local cricket team, Monkwearmouth, where he drew large crowds and excelled at fielding as well as bowling and batting. The showman's humour that he showed on the football field was also deployed to entertain the fans on the cricket pitch, where he would pretend to miss slip catches, and then look behind him as if the ball was speeding to the boundary - before fishing the ball out of his pocket. But in the final analysis he was said to have thought that cricket was a game that took too long, and to have regarded it mainly as a good way to keep fit.

Tennis was not as popular in the 1950s as today, and he did not play it until he was about twenty five - when on holiday with a Scottish international footballer, Jimmy Stephen. Stephen was a good tennis player and asked Shack to join him in an open competition. Shack told him that he never played the game but would have a try. After a few exploratory hits over the net he started to get a feel for the game, and, learning the rules as he played, he went on to win the competition.

At squash and badminton he was equally adept and was even offered work as a professional baseball player in the US after his ankle injury forced him out of football. It was an offer he did not consider, as it would have taken him away from his beloved north east.

Another skill he was surprised to discover later was in shooting moving targets. He used to go shooting with a friend who had won medals in his time in the armed forces, and so could hit any target, or at least any static target. But when it came to shooting rabbits his friend was hopeless while Shack turned out to be natural. He had two advantages. He could follow the rabbits while they were moving; and when they stopped to listen for danger his reflexes were quick enough to shoot immediately before they moved off again.

On the more trivial side, he was known for playing tricks with coins. One was a trick introduced by Don Revie when he joined Sunderland. It was to throw a sixpence a few feet into the air, catch it on his instep, flick it up into the air again and catch it in his jacket pocket. Shack had, like many other people, taken a dislike to Revie and went home to practise it alone. Then a few days later he demonstrated an improved version, throwing the sixpence up to the ceiling rather than just a few feet in the air, to upstage Revie. He later repeated the trick on TV at the time of his retirement.

The most extraordinary of all his tricks, however, was with a golf club. He had found that he was not as gifted at games where the ball was static when hit, and although he eventually ended up with a handicap of about six he did not really excel at golf. But what he could do was throw a golf ball up in the air and then, bringing down his throwing arm to grasp the club with both hands, drive it on the half-volley straight down the middle of the fairway and further than good club players could hit it off the tee.

But Shack's football skill was not all god-given natural ability. Billy Bingham observed that Shack, who was sometimes accused of laziness, in fact worked at improving his football with a surprising intensity. In particular, Bingham attributed

Shack's ball control partly to the game of "football-tennis" that they had devised in Sunderland's gymnasium.

Some of the players, including Shack's good friend Ray Daniel, were not enamored of the time-worn methods of fitness training, which included starting with laps round the pitch. Daniel, who was as disrespectful of club directors as Shack, is supposed to have asked the team's chairman, Billy Ditchburn, when he made a visit to a training session, "Mr Chairman, could you tell me if this red stuff (the red cinders on the track surrounding the pitch) goes all the way round to the other side?"

The top players felt they got more out of football-tennis, in which the rules were that the ball could be hit over the net with any part of the body except for hands and arms. It was made more challenging by the rule that a return that hit the gymnasium wall was still in play. Shack was said to be able to bring down the ball at shoulder height, using his leg as if it were a prehensile arm. There are obvious similarities with Brazilian beach tennis where the players (women as well as men) never let the ball touch the sand, catching it on their heads, chests, shoulders, thighs and insteps before returning it over the net – and are probably the most skillful football players in the world. Or an even more memorable game I once saw in an African village where the players never let the ball touch the bumpy ground, trapping the ball in mid air and juggling it on their feet, thighs and heads before passing it on.

Shack, however, did not really have "tricks" like some other stars. Once, when sharing a room with Stanley Matthews before playing in an international, Shack was amazed when he picked up his room-mate's daytime shoes to find that they were unexpectedly heavy. He apparently weighted them down with metal so that that when he changed into his football boots he felt light-footed.

But although Shack did not adopt any similar practices, fellow players remarked on two physical oddities: he had exceptionally long feet and toes (he was about 5'8" and wore size tens) and he often wore rugby boots which gave a better feel for the ball than the hard reinforced toe caps of 1940s football boots.

12

The Footballers Turn To Crime in a Grey Economy

Although the maximum wage was not officially abolished until 1961, under the counter payments had mushroomed after the war.

It is well known that Shack was offered an unauthorised payment as early as 1946, after learning (from the newspapers) that he had just been sold to Newcastle United for £13,000. He admitted his malfeasance in his book, revealing that he had asked a Newcastle director how much he would get out of the deal. He was promised £500, fifty times the official FA signing on fee of £10. It would seem inconceivable that he did not know that this was illegal, having already been a professional footballer for six years.

In fact since the 1940s it had been common knowledge that it would be difficult to attract and retain good players without under the counter payments. Some were straightforward financial payments, but others were not. They might take the form of subsidised housing, gifts for the players, jewelry for their wives or payments for a second job, real or otherwise.

A high profile example was that of Trevor Ford, who was transferred to Sunderland for £30,000 in 1950. Previuosly, however, he had considered joining Chelsea, where he had asked the Chelsea management about the possibility of having a part time job there to supplement his income. The Chelsea Chairman reported him to the FA and he was fined £100. The subject was made public in 1957 in Ford's autobiography "I Lead the Attack" in which the first chapter was called "Under the Counter", and he wat not contrite. He argued that most footballers were breaking the law to get cash illegally, becoming 'undesirables' as a direct consequence of the niggardly maximum wage.

Ford became, like Shack, a crusader for reform and went on to support a proposal by Manchester City's Chairman Bob Smith to grant an amnesty over illegal payments while the whole subject of a footballer's maximum wages was reviewed. Ford had made the case in his book that "the rules had made criminals out of players". But the proposed amnesty was rejected by the clubs.

The illegal practices, however, did not really hit the headlines until 1957, when Shack's own club, Sunderland, was accused of multiple offences.

In retrospect Sunderland would always have been suspect. They had spent more than any other club on transfer s to assemble their team of all talents - a set of stars who in theory would only be paid the maximum wage. And the club were still paying out throughout the 1950s on players like Trevor Ford, the most expensive player in the country at £30,000, Ken Chisholm for £15,000 and Ted Purdon, also £15,000.

When the accusation of undeclared payments came it was in a mysterious form. It was made in a letter to the Football League authorities signed by a "Mr Smith" and containing a wealth of details, the Daily Express commenting that "Smith gives enough facts to show he is well acquainted with the Sunderland club and that his object is the punishment of individuals".

The identity of Mr Smith has never been revealed, but one possibility is that it was a Sunderland director with a grudge after an internal power struggle. The directors at the time were EW Ditchburn (Chairman), Col J Turnbull, S Ritson (Vice Chairman), LW Evans, SS Collings, J Reed, WS Martin and J Parker; and the Daily Express claimed that in one of the letters to the Football League two of the Directors had threatened to demand an inquiry unless two of their fellow directors resigned. Another possibility was that the culprit was a player envious of the extra payments paid to some but not all of the team.

The result was an inquiry, initiated by Alan Hardaker, the Secretary of the Football League. At first it got nowhere and the investigators considered abandoning the case. Then in March 1957 a commission of six members of the Football Association and the Football League summoned Sunderland's chairman and manager to a hearing, and followed up by summoning the whole board. A few weeks later they publicised the results of a report.

The findings were sensational and made national headlines. After uncovering little evidence at first, some further sleuthing by the investigators revealed that the club's accounts included a suspiciously high price for deliveries of straw - which, before undersoil heating was introduced, was used to cover the pitch in the winter months to protect it from snow and ice. Sunderland were found to have placed orders far in excess of what was needed, and the suppliers had then given the club credit notes for the amounts that were returned. The board would then cash the credit notes and use the money to make additional payments to the players, none of which were shown in the books. The scam had been going on for five years and the fraud amounted to £5,217. Ted Ditchburn the Sunderland Chairman at the time admitted sole responsibility although he disclosed that his close friend Bill Martin also knew about it. In fact, Ditchburn fearing being found out had paid £2,700 back into the club's accounts to try to hide some of the illegal payments.

The club was fined £5000 and four of the directors were banned from football sine die (i.e. with no date set for further consideration).

Many supporters were sympathetic to the club. First, they reasoned that the directors were just doing what was necessary to keep their players reasonably rewarded in the increasingly grey market that was footballers' wages. It had been unrealistic to expect to pay a player who had just been bought for £20-30,000 a signing on fee of only £10 – a figure that had been agreed in the 1890s by a Football Association steeped in the Corinthian ideal of amateur sport, disapproving of payments to professionals.

Secondly, other clubs were almost certainly making the same sort of payments.

And, thirdly, the Sunderland chairman was not a shady character: on the contrary, he was a local businessman who was devoted to his club and popular with both the players and workers at his furniture factory. He lacked airs and graces, often being seen driving his pink Rolls Royce down to the fish and chip shop. Also, he presided over a happy club. Trevor Ford describes how he found the officials and the playing staff ... "If ever a player felt wanted it was at Sunderland. Life off the field of play was serene and sweet, with no petty regulations, no worries and no back stabbing. If ever I wanted a drink or a smoke I didn't have to do it in private ... I had not been there long before one of the directors found me a job as a car salesman for his firm ... I was already settled in one of the club houses, a good-class semi in a good-class district and all I paid for it was thirty bob a week ... What a contrast to some clubs!" But this was possible only because they had broken the rules (and before Ford's difficulties with Shack).

Then there were further punishments. Six Sunderland players were accused by the FA of receiving illegal signing-on payments and five of them were hauled in front of an FA Commission to answer questions. They were Ray Daniel, Willie Fraser, Ken Chisholm, Billy Elliott and Johnny Hannigan; but on the instructions of their union's solicitor, George Davies, they all remained silent. Consequently, they were all suspended for life, sine die. There was, however a good reason for their remaining silent. George Davies' company had unearthed the fact that the FA and the Football League did not have the legal power to set up such a commission or to suspend players or directors for life. So all the suspensions – of players and directors – were later revoked. The whole incident had shown up the authorities in a bad light. They had accused players of practices that there well known to be widespread throughout the country, and were a consequence not so much of dishonesty as of the antiquated control of wages imposed by the authorities. That is to say, it was seen that it was the authorities, not the players, who were at fault, and that they had tried to assume powers that they did not have.

Meanwhile Trevor Ford had refused to retract the allegations he made in his autobiography and was banned sine die by the Football League. But this ban was also lifted and Ford subsequently signed for PSV Eindhoven in the Netherlands.

Bill Murray the Sunderland Manager was also given a fine of £200 and a month later he resigned, after 28 years with the club. The rest of the Board was severely censured.

The punishments, however, were short lived. After it had been established that the FA did not have the rights to impose these sanctions, almost all them were rescinded.

It was too late for Bill Murray who died two years after he was forced out. And also for the Chairman. Ditchburn had been deeply upset by his lifetime ban. When it was lifted he was given £650 compensation in an out of court settlement, and he hoped to return to the Sunderland board. But he found that the other directors blocked him, and at the age of 74 he was out of the club to which he had devoted his life for ever. He, like Bill Murray, died soon afterwards.

Against this background the Players Union was become increasingly determined to end the need for players to break the law in order to be paid a reasonable wage. They cited comparisons with wages abroad: for example Eddie Firmani had just been transferred from Charlton Athletic to Sampdoria in Italy, for a lump sum of £5,000, a wage of £100 per week, use of a luxury flat and freedom to move after two years.

The union's new Chairman, Jimmy Hill, started touring the country to campaign for an amnesty for all footballers who confessed to having received payments under the counter. But he was only modestly successful, with the vast majority of professional footballers unwilling to take the risk of the consequences of admitting to 'crimes'.

What was Shack's role in all this? He had railed against the maximum wage, the meanness of football directors and the feudal nature of the players' contracts in his book, but by 1957 he was lying low. In fact when most of the Sunderland players decided to sign Jimmy Hill's petition, Shack refused to support the union's approach, and accounts are divided on whether this led to a falling out in the dressing room. Once again, Shack did it his way, arguing that the right approach to pay was a strike. And he may have been right, as the eventual victory of the players union was achieved by the threat of a strike. The nature of Shack's involvement possibly showed only an awkward squad desire to do things his way and not go along with the crowd. He was also close to retirement.

13

The Book

Shack's book, The Clown Prince of Soccer, was published in 1955. It was edited by David R Jack, a friend and journalist who also wrote books about Matt Busby and Jimmy McIlroy of Burnley. He used to visit Shack's family home in Seaburn to work on the draft over weekends.

By far the most inflammatory part of the book was the blank page under the title "The average director's knowledge of football", with a footnote that "this chapter has deliberately been left blank in accordance with the author's wishes". Shack explained in an interview how it came about. After putting in some long hours writing, they were just about to go out for a break when Shack dropped a blank sheet of paper on to the table. David asked what it was for and Shack replied that it was the average director's knowledge of football. It was an offhand comment, but Jack had a journalist's killer instinct for a sensation and persuaded Shack to include it in the book.

It was published by Nicholas Kaye of London and sold out quickly, with long queues outside Arrowsmiths, the local bookshop. It went through five editions between September and Christmas.

Its contents were a mixture of autobiographical chapters alternating with a hard hitting critique of the state of football and the staid, pompous and self-important officials that ran the game in the 1950s. It was a courageous book to write before the end of his career. He was only thirty-three at the time and had been playing for England only the year before he published. But he did not pull his punches, risking his livelihood. His main targets were:

1. The 'player's contract' that tied him to the club, effectively in perpetuity if the club so wished.
2. The low wages of footballers, and the fact that they were controlled, while other sportsmen and entertainers like boxers

and actors were paid according to the crowds they could attract.
3. Transfers that were arranged by the clubs and in which the players often had little say.
4. The ignorance of football club directors.
5. The incompetence of the England selectors.
6. The meanness and class consciousness of the managers and selectors.

The Players Contract

Shack tore into the player's contract in Chapter 2 of his book. He expressed amazement that the standard contract that tied a footballer to the club for life, but could be terminated without notice (although only by the club, not by the player) had survived into the 1950s.

"No more one sided agreement was ever fashioned" he wrote, than this "evil document ... a canker".

He went on to argue that professional footballers were effectively puppets, serfs, slaves. Even the footballing greats of the era, such a Tom Finney and Wilk Mannion, who had been offered well paid jobs at top teams in Europe, were prisoners. Both asked for transfers abroad but were rejected. "Why should we sell our best player?" was the cold response.

"All the trump cards", Shack argued, "were in one hand ... No other form of civil employment places such restrictions on the movement of individuals, while at the same time retaining the power to dismiss them summarily."

The players' union had been lobbying for reforms for years but their suggestions had been "scorned ... at every frustrating meeting with the tradition-bound rulers of football ... The staid gentry of Preston and Lancaster Gate."

The small print in the contracts was even more insulting. The 'neat little coloured book' that had to be 'carried at all times' forbade dancing between Wednesdays and Saturdays, spending a weekend away from home or residing in a place not approved by the club. Shack called the little book the Seventeen Pillars of Serfdom.

The final insult was eviction from the clubs' houses when the player retired, typically around the age of 35 (few people owned their houses in the 1950s).

He did not, however, raise the subject of the role of the upper echelons of society in setting these rules back in the 1890s (see chapter ...). Had he been familiar with the social history behind the set-up Shack may well have been even more outraged. He might have observed that even maids in the Victorian mansions of the gentlemen who had laid out the rules for professional football clubs had the right to leave.

He was also too early to appeal to the European Union's constitution which later gave citizens the right to move freely to seek employment wherever they wanted. The UK did not join the EU until eighteen years after the book was written, and it took another twenty two years for the Bosman ruling to be able to exploit the EU rules on freedom of movement for workers, and to loosen up the clubs' control of their players even further.

Wages

Shack was not particularly critical of the maximum wage per se. It was £15 a week in 1955, and he considered it not too unreasonable - at least until you took into account the facts that only a quarter of professional footballers got the maximum and that a career in football was usually short (averaging seven years, he suggested, although most of Sunderland's team of talents did not retire until their mid-thirties). He even conceded in his later book, "The Return of the Clown Prince", that "I can have no complaints about what football gave to me and my family" (this was in the context of writing about his enjoyable tour of East Africa, playing exhibition games and coaching).

His main argument was more fundamental: it was that any wage control was an anomaly; that football was alone in not paying its best performers according to their talents. He referred to the high incomes of Rocky Marciano, the top boxer at the time, Sir

Gordon Richards, the top jockey and Tommy Trinder, a popular comedian. Who, he asked would expect the star of South Pacific to be paid the same as the girl extras lying on the beach?

He considered the parsimony of the clubs inexcusable, given that football was the greatest entertainment money spinner in England.

He might also have queried the right of the Football Association, as self-appointed authority, to fix wages.

He dismissed another argument that had been used to justify wage control: that it was a team game. Shack pointed to examples of high wages for other types of stars being consistent with team efforts, for example in stage shows.

The players' payments for big games also attracted his anger. The Cup Final was one the great social events of the 1950s, being attended by the King, but the players were paid less than one per cent of the gate money – plus a similar sum for the winning team, and none for the losers.

At internationals it was almost as bad. Although the players were paid £50 per appearance this amounted to only about two per cent of the takings of around £50,000.

Transfers

Shack called the transfers of footballers in the 1950s "public auctions of human beings." He likened them to sales of slaves in Arabia and North Africa.

Shack's own experiences had been typical. As will be recalled from Chapter 7, he had not been informed that a move was on the cards when he was first transferred, from Bradford Park Avenue to Newcastle United,; and he was not in the room when the negotiation of the £13,000 fee took place. The big money in football was that paid by clubs to clubs, not clubs to players.

Other top players had the same experience. When Danny Blanchflower was transferred from Barnsley to Aston Villa in 1951 he was taken to a hotel out of town and then to a hotel kitchen downstairs to get something to eat while Barnsley's chairman - Joe Richards, later to become the chairman of the Football League -

went upstairs to a proper dining room to negotiate the deal with the mystery club. It was only after the event that Blanchflower was informed that he had been sold to Aston Villa (see Chapter 18 for more details of the dismissive way in which the highly intelligent Blanchflower was treated and later had his revenge).

Gary Imlach described the transfer of his father, Stewart Imlach, a Scottish international, from Luton to Coventry in 1960 in similar terms. "My father was roused from his bed around 1 am to be informed that he had been sold." Imlach pictured the scene ... "fresh brandies ordered despite the bar being officially closed, cigars newly lit, (the directors) perhaps on first name terms now: Well I think we have a deal. Shall we get him up?" He added "Only after a deal had been struck was the merchandise produced." Imlach's experience of an earlier transfer, from Bury to Derby County in 1954 had been even more dispiriting. He was told that Derby had offered £7,500 for him, but he was getting married in two months, and would naturally want to discuss an unanticipated move to another town with his fiancé. But he knew the reality: if they wanted to sell you that was it; if you resisted they would have cut your pay for the next season and put you on the transfer list. So he signed: no private discussion with his fiancée, no face to face meeting with his manager, no trip to see his future club.

However, Shack did miss one obvious point in his book. In what other profession is a transfer fee paid to the company rather than the worker when he changes jobs? Could you imagine a film company securing George Clooney's services by paying his current employer a multi-million pound transfer fee and paying George Clooney a £10 signing on fee?

Football Club Directors

After the famous blank page about "the average director's knowledge of football" Shack went on (in his Chapter 16) to dismiss club *managers* as being "glorified office boys who bow and scrape... while directors, usually unsuccessfully, perform the managerial functions". Club managers in the 1950s clearly had a different role from today's high profile versions.

In fact he does not say much else about directors, except that the players had good fun exchanging stories about the directors' limited knowledge of the game. He recalls being asked by a director who came into the dressing room if his 'spikes' were comfortable; and another who watched Arsenal playing was enthusing about his team's performance until it was pointed out that they, as the away team, were playing in white rather than their usual red.

Shack's views on football managers were echoed by Danny Blanchflower, another of the new wave of articulate footballers. As soon as he had arrived in England from Northern Ireland to play for Barnsley he had signed on to train as an accountant at a local technical college. He found the football club managers of the 1950s insular and parochial. He particularly deplored the focus on long runs for fitness ("no brain work or ball work"), the rigid "five forwards and two backs" formations of the 1950s and the managers' lack of authority. Many of them did not have a final say on team selection and could be over-ruled by the directors. Danny Blanchflower's biography refers to a 1962 film, The Saturday Men It was about day to day operations at a top club (West Bromwich Albion), and showed the club manager being treated like a second class citizen at a board meeting.

England selectors

It was in Chapter 6 that he targeted his great bête noir, the England selectors - "the blackest n****r in the woodpile[8], the biggest fly in the ointment, the ever present ball and chain restricting the efforts of the England team".

He listed them: Mr Arthur Drewry who had connections with the fishing industry in Grimsby; Mr Harold Shentall, a wholesale provisions merchant from Chesterfield; Mr Harry Rench, a

---

[8] Oops. This was, however, a common expression in the 1950s, and Shack in fact wrote with great warmth about his tour of East Africa and playing local teams.

wholesale greengrocer from Middlesbrough; Sir Amos Brookhurst, a Huddersfield solicitor. Shack observed that what this predominantly northern group had in common was an absence of soccer-playing background, except for one who once played in goal for an amateur team. He went on: "I mean no disrespect when I suggest that the selectors would be better selectors of cabbages and gorgonzola than players ... Is it unreasonable to suggest that the selectors' credentials should be based on soccer skill, rather than on fish, fruit or flour?" He recalled how they played club centre forwards on the wing and wingers on the wrong wing for England.

Again, Danny Blanchflower had equally dismissive reactions to the selectors when he first played for Northern Ireland a few years later. He was, of course, proud to represent his country, and had "borrowed and bought clothing coupons for a suit for the occasion". But he was disappointed by his exposure to his masters on the boat to England. He considered most of them to be fools, to the extent that it undermined his pride at representing his country: "Where is the honour in playing for a shambles, an outfit that stands for nothing save inefficiency and hypocrisy?" He concluded that international football seemed to be run for the benefit of the committee men rather than the players and supporters.

Meanness and class consciousness of managers and selectors

The book lists many examples, large and small, of the meanness and class consciousness of the managers, directors and selectors in English football. They include:

- Third class rail tickets for players and first class tickets for managers and selectors.
- International players sometimes having to stand most the way to Scotland.
- The players not being allowed to keep their shirts after a game
- The FA's refusal of Shack's request for a ticket for the 1954 Cup Final the day after he played in a match for England.

Fortunately, he was able to get a couple of tickets from a friend in 'the fishery business', that is to say, a wealthy businessman of the type that would have no difficulty in getting tickets.

- Players' wives being allocated separate tickets all over the ground, with some not under cover, to watch their husbands playing in the 1951 Cup Final for Newcastle United. They had been promised tickets together near the Royal Box to see their husbands troop up to shake hands with the King after the game. Only when the players threatened to strike were the tickets replaced by a set sitting together near the royal box.
- The attempt of Sir Stanley Rous, the arrogant pro-apartheid Secretary of the English Football Association, to prevent Shack accepting an invitation to visit Kenya to play exhibition matches and help with coaching in the summer break. The letter sent by Rous to the Kenyan FA after the publication of Shack's book contained the following extraordinary words:

Sir Stanley Rous
The Football association
Patron:
Her Majesty the Queen

To: *22 Lancaster Gate:*
J H Wittingham *London W2*
The FA of Kenya
PO Box234
Nairobi *27th October 1955*

Dear Mr Wittingham,

... We are not sure whether we will give permission for Mr Shackleton to act as a coach to your Association in view of his attitude to governing bodies ...

Yours sincerely,
S Rous,
Secretary

Shack compared the distant, patrician attitude of Rous with that of Leo Blunt, the Secretary of the Netherlands Football Association, who on the last day of a tour of Holland called in on the Sunderland team. Arriving at the hotel and finding the players with no plans to go out and explore Amsterdam he realised that they were short of funds, and took them all out to the city's best restaurant and night club.

His main target, however, was the Jubilee Benevolent Fund. It was set up in 1938 to help footballers who had fallen on hard times after their playing days were finished. By 1947 the fund had reached £47,000. But, extraordinarily, it had made only eight pay-outs in nine years. Attempting to justify this, a Football League spokesman suggested that "it is a healthy sign that there have been so few applications from players for assistance."

Even worse, the patrician organisers of the fund had rejected an offer from the football pool firms of another £100,000 over twenty years. They turned it down because it was 'tainted' money, from gambling.

* * *

Although intelligent, penetrating and strengthened by barbed humour Shack's critique was not strident. At the end of the key Chapter 2 he writes "while apologising if this chapter delves too deeply into the 'politics' of football I am sure that the question of players' working conditions badly needs airing ... I have tried to put forward a reasonable case, and I hope I have succeeded."

* * *

A third big theme in his book was his being ignored by the England selectors for most of his playing years. Both the first *and* the last chapters of his book are about his rejection. Chapter 1 is entitled "'Resurrected by England selectors". He writes that at the age of thirty-two and out of the team for five years he was unexpectedly recalled to play for his country – but almost turned the offer down.

He had been saddened by England's steady decline since he last played, including their humiliating elimination from the 1950 World Cup in the first round by the USA and the 7-1 and 6-3 defeats by Hungary in 1953. He wrote that "it was like watching a house burn down and being denied the right to contribute the bucket of water in my hand". He also noted that another great ball player and individualist, Stanley Matthews, had been treated the same way, having been dropped in his thirties and recalled only when he was forty. Shack believed that this reflected the selectors' preference for players who would get rid of the ball quickly rather than players who could beat an opponent.

He had been particularly disappointed to have been excluded from the 1954 World Cup after years of stellar performances at Sunderland. He told his wife that "if the selectors call me after this.. I won't bother to play." Later, the heading of Chapter 6 of his book was "I never want to play for England again."

But he did play. He claimed that two things changed his mind. The first was typical Shack: that he was opening a hairdressing salon at the time and the publicity from playing for England would give the business a good send-off. And secondly, after being after excluded for the World Cup squad, he was motivated by the chance of facing West Germany just a few months after they had become the champions.

And he played well, scoring an exceptional goal. Then he was dropped and never played again.

The last chapter of his book returns to the subject of his being frozen out by England's selectors. It doesn't say much, but he leaves the impression that the wound was festering

14
Reactions to the Book

The book was a sensation, and the reviews were very positive. They included:

"This is easily the best book yet by a footballer and Shackleton may have done the game a service by putting into print what so many players think." **(Aberdeen Press and Journal)**

* * *

"Professor Len Shackleton, the Sunderland and England wayside genius, who split the soccer atom in his sensational book, finds himself scorched by the flames of his own honesty. His outspoken comment on the game has raised a real rumpus and revealed the jester as a challenging champion of the rights of professional footballers." **(Sunday Pictorial)**

* * *

"Len Shackleton erstwhile England inside forward – he never wants to play for England again – has written the most bitter attack on soccer I have ever read." **(Daily Mail)**

* * *

"Shackleton is right to have seen that his book is written this way. He has said things that will not please a good many people but it is certainly time that they were said." **(Sports Express)**

* * *

"All the critics seem to have forgotten one thing, that in his book Len really tries to do something for Britain's national game. He reveals abuses and neglect which show why Britain's reputation is now so low among football nations" **(Sunday Sun, 1955)**

* * *

"Points that Shack puts forward about coaching are that great players who cannot talk will not do; nor will great talkers who cannot play. Shack has certainly proved that he is in neither of these categories." **(Reynolds News)**

But some readers, as well as some non-readers, were predictably outraged. The Daily Mail invited responses to *their own review of the book* (the third quoted at the beginning of this chapter), and were rewarded with the following, all written *before they had read it*:

".. the fact that Shackleton has two successful confectionery businesses and is now branching out into hairdressing should be sufficient answer in itself to criticism of football directors who have never kicked a ball. Has he ever made a toffee apple or cut a lock of hair?" **(H Fay, Liverpool)**

* * *

"Shackleton has been a fortunate young man – he has set up three businesses on money received from the game which *directors, the object of his scorn, help to finance.* If he had been on active service during the war he would have had many shocks far worse than descending a coal mine and he might never have returned to play football – or write a book." **(A E Shuttleworth, Shipley, Yorkshire).**

* * *

Best of all, however, was the response of a football club director, apoplectic at the blank page that was Chapter 9:

"Mr Shackleton,

First of all I would like to associate myself with those 'fans' of whom you say: 'They called me the clown prince of football. They called me irresponsible. They called me bighead...'
But, believe me, I'm no fan of yours.

Like you, Mr Shackleton, I have earned my bread and butter as a professional footballer and was proud to do so. ... There's an old saying about 'biting the hand'. Remember it?

.. I feel just as proud of being an 'average director' ... I have been on both sides of the fence ... forgive me then if I assume that I do know a little more about these things than even you ...

But ask yourself, Mr Shackleton, does your prominence in the game give you the right to be unpardonably rude to those 'average directors', the men whose interest in football and footballers has, no doubt, helped in some measure to your present influence in the business world.

I can tell you that it isn't necessary to have been a footballer to become a successful director ...

Directors provide for the club the most important thing of all.. the cash to enable it to carry on ... And *you don't*, the sportsmen who are *continually dipping their hands into their (the directors') pockets...*

.. Without the average director, there would be no need for the Shackletons or the rest. There just would not be any League football clubs. ...." **(Jack Diffin)**

15
What Was He Like: Clown Or Devil?

A faded photograph of Shackleton's father gives few clues to his personality, or to the effect it might have had on Len's life. It shows a small man in a suit looking rather bewildered in front of the camera.

In fact his father had been a good sportsman and in particular a good footballer. But not in the style of his son. His father had not been a dribbler: he had been a pitbull terrier known for crunching tackles, and Shack speculated that he would have been a better footballer if he had had more of the "devil" of his father. He may have been right in the physical sense: Shack was not a great tackler. But in the way he lived his professional life he may have had more devil in him than was good for him.

Although his father had hopes of becoming a professional footballer, he eventually became a painter and decorator. It seems likely that the relationship between father and son was typical of the time – more distant than today's, with most of the upbringing of children left to the mother. Shack's few references to his father suggest that he had the Yorkshire traits of bluntness and no-nonsense straight talking: praise did not come easily to him. It also seems likely that their relationship was similar to that described wonderfully in Duncan Hamilton's 'pitch perfect' book, The Footballer Who Could Fly, in which he observes that "without football we were strangers under a shared roof. With it, we were father and son."

Shack had known what he wanted to be from at an early age. When the children were asked at Sunday school about the profession they would choose when they grew up, Shack said that he was going to be a footballer. The teacher disapproved, telling young Len it was not a career, that footballers only become professionals when they couldn't get a proper job. Worse, if he was a footballer he would find himself "mixing with *all kinds of people*". (Twenty years later Shack was to say that having mixed with many kinds of people the most genuine and loyal friends were professional footballers.) "Far from being a dead-end occupation for street corner boys and snooker saloon spivs" he listed footballers that were successful in education, business and the arts.

Small and apparently frail as he was, Len had a definite mind of his own by the time he reached his teenage years, and it was not always to his advantage. Chapter two describes how at the age of sixteen, having realized a dream by being taken on to the staff of Arsenal, the best team in the country, he more or less threw it all away when the club manager stopped him and asked him to tie his shoelaces. "Tie them yourself" was Shack's (or his devil's) reply and a few months later he was sacked.

He was deeply hurt by his rejection. He devoted nine pages of his autobiography to his few months at Arsenal, including how he was patronised by the manager George Allison on the day of his dismissal by being shown a modern TV, so that he could tell the primitive folks back in Yorkshire about the wonders of modern science. He knew that he was good but he admitted that he had been humiliated at Arsenal. He didn't yet have the strength to get a corner kick over to the six yard area. . He wrote "Yes I can joke about my Arsenal days now, but it was not very funny in 1939. I was out of a job and faced the prospect of crawling home as a football failure after leaving to a fanfare of trumpets."

At this low point in his life Shack was not quite confident that his unusual talent was going to guarantee success. But within two years of the end of the war he was playing for England and Newcastle United. And by then he was not going to be pushed around as at Arsenal. His 'agin the government' nature and determination to fight for his rights led to battles with the directors, especially over the club's failure to provide the accommodation he had been promised when he signed on. Called into the boardroom to make his case he was outwitted by one of the well-spoken directors and retired humiliated. Shack probably assumed that it was his lack of formal education that had hobbled him. In fact he never ha much of a chance: his adversary had been a formidable barrister, William McKeag.

Shack was never happy at Newcastle. It was only when he moved across the Tyne to join Sunderland that he finally settled, playing there until he retired. He loved the north east and stayed there until he moved late in life to Cumbria to be near his wife's sister.

At Sunderland, Billy Bingham, the Irish international and, later, manager, who played alongside Shack for seven years, remembered him being "as quick witted off the field as he was on it." And Brian Redhead also called him a "man of immense wit". He remembered how "I once saw him take a penalty against Manchester City when Frank Swift was still alive. He put the ball on the penalty spot and then walked almost to the half way line. Then he ran like a train at the ball, took a tremendous kick and Swift dived. But the ball was still on the spot: he hadn't touched it. Then he turned round and back heeled it into the net … Swift walked out, took Shackleton's head between those great hands and kissed him.

He also liked to joke with the crowd. An old Sunderland supporter remembered a Saturday afternoon when Shack was waiting to take a throw-in near the corner flag. He turned to them and said: "Enjoying the game, boys?" Then he asked them the time.

"About three minutes to go, Shack."

"OK," said Shack. "Do you think there's time for another one?"

"Ye-e-s" they shouted. And Shack threw the ball in, collected a pass, dribbled into the penalty area and scored another one.

Bingham thought Shack cared much more than his clowning suggested. Like the good poker player that he was, Shack didn't show what was on his mind. He probably took criticism much more to heart that you could gauge from his posing as the clown prince – in particular over his being ignored by England. Bingham also described the one of the few games where Shack really disgraced himself – a cup-tie against Swansea Town. Shack played poorly and seemed to be making little effort (in fact he was not feeling well). The crowd actually booed him. After the game Bill Murray appeared in the dressing room and tore into him. Shack just looked unaffected, staring at the floor as Murray continued. When Murray's tirade stopped Shack looked up, rubbed his ear with his towel and said, looking puzzled "Eh? You what?" In fact it upset him so much that he wrote a chapter about it in his book. He was dropped for the next game, but a few weeks later he was once again on top form for the first team.

He was also modest in his demeanour. After scoring a wonderful goal Shack would amble back to the centre circle, expressionless and head down – very unlike the triumphalist Ronaldo slide.

Shack dominated conversation in the dressing room with his good humour, and Stan Anderson remembered how he was liked not only by the older stars but also by the younger players whom he encouraged and showed around when they were away from home, seeming to know all the best places to go.

He was also the centre of their off-duty social life. In those days, before they had fast cars, new hairstyles, tattoos and racehorses to fill their time, the footballers spent long hours playing cards, mainly poker and three card brag, the simpler poor man's version of poker.

The stakes were high – sometimes over three times the weekly maximum wage - and Shack usually won.

A typical photograph of the time shows three internationals - Shack, Ray Daniels and Billy Elliott - sitting over a poker hand, all three with cigarettes in their fingers, which may well have been brown with the nicotine stains that were common before filters came in. Ray Daniels is wearing a smart suit and tie, with a modern hairstyle; Shack looks more old-fashioned with a club tie and a cardigan underneath his blazer; and Elliott looks like the gunslinger he was. I have a vivid memory of Elliott late one foggy Saturday afternoon straddling a full back who had tackled him and thumping him again and again, his arm going like a piston. Shack regarded him as the hardest player in the league – hard being a highly complimentary term in the north east of the 1950s, both on the football field and in everyday life. Billy Elliott was the Joey Barton of his time.

Only occasionally did Shack join the bridge table of Willie Watson, the double international at football and cricket, and he found it hard going.

By their friends ye shall know them, and Shack's friends were the wits and jokers.

His best friend and roommate was Ray Daniels, the Welsh international centre half. Tall, handsome and elegantly dressed he was a good mimic and singer, his favourite song being the Red Flag. Known for his less than respectful attitude towards the management and the weakness of his enthusiasm for training, he used to claim that he had never actually completed a training lap round the pitch, asking the club officials "what's it like on the other side of the pitch?"

He played for Sunderland for four years, and although an unusually good ball player for a centre half he was capable of mistakes. His end came with the exit of the respected manager, Bill Murray, who was forced to retire after the under the counter payments scandal. While Bill Murray had been tactful and well-liked the new manager, Alan Brown, was a driven fitness fanatic. On the first day he assembled the players, pointed to the balls lying at the other end of the pitch and asked four players to go and fetch them. They happened to be Shack, Billy Elliott, Ray Daniel and Don Revie, all of whom were strong characters not to be ordered around. They trooped off reluctantly with Ray Daniels in particular taking his time to return. Later Brown had them running for half an hour and then challenged them to beat him in two fast last laps at the end (he came in about sixth). Ray left Sunderland soon afterwards.

Shack was also lukewarm about traditional training. Rather than run hard to build stamina he used to run round the pitch keeping the ball in the air the whole time.

The day Brown after asked him to retrieve the balls, Shack told the club that he had had a flare up of an old ankle injury on the first day of the season; and he never played again.

Other great friends included Ken Chisholm, a Scot who was an ex-RAF officer, and much more glamorous that the typical 1950s footballer. He gave parties that were attended by show girls from the Sunderland Empire, and Shack used to tell him that he would not have wanted him to be married to his sister. Another friend was Ted Purdon, a big handsome fair-haired South African.

The nuances of the personalities of the foursome – Shack, Daniels, Chisholm and Purdon - can be inferred from Shack's recollections of a visit to New York on a close season tour in 1956. It started with a disaster in the first few days when Purdon lost most of his money on an ill-advised walk around Harlem on his own. But they discovered that they could sell blood at $10 a session, and Purdon and Chisholm went back day after day, giving different false names each time, to recoup the lost money.

While they were there Shack was fascinated by Chisholm's and Purdon's facility with girls. The pair managed to get invited to parties with film stars, and Chisholm struck up an unlikely friendship with Marilyn Monroe who frequented a café close to where they were staying. Purdon even had a date with Joan Crawford. Shack, deeply impressed, could only conclude that people either have 'it' or they don't, and those who don't can only stand and admire.

Shack had his faults, and could occasionally be spiteful. Billy Bingham speculated that one of the reasons he got on badly with Sunderland's centre forward, Trevor Ford. was that Ford was good looking and was continually combing his hair in the mirror in the changing room. He also photographed well in evening dress. Shack also thought Ford was 'in with the directors', who had found him a nice white collar part time job as the manager of a car salesroom during his time at Sunderland.

Another player about whom he had reservations was Don Revie, who was called Billy Graham because of his preaching about the virtues of clean living – no smoking, drinking or swearing. Shack went to some lengths to upstage him in public, practising tricks that Revie was particularly proud of and doing them better.

He also more or less blackmailed Syd Collings, the Sunderland director, in public, to get a benefit match on which the board was dragging its feet. Benefit matches were important for footballers, setting them up with nest eggs at the end of their playing careers, but the clubs were often slow to come forward.

A dreadful example was the refusal of vindictive directors at Newcastle to give Frank Brennan, a highly popular centre half, a benefit match at St James' Park. Similarly, Shack, when faced with similar resistance, hinted to Collings that the Football League might be interested in the possibility that he might have been involved in under-the-counter payments of the type that had seen his fellow directors ruined. He did so in the presence of other players; Collings apparently went red and the benefits match was arranged at short notice.

Shack could also be cutting at times: he claimed that Paul Gascoigne was the only player he'd ever pay to see as he was the only one who almost as talented as he was.

But these were exceptions. I asked a cousin of mine who had lived in the north east most of his life (he became the vice Chancellor of Northumbria University) if he had ever met Shack.

"Yes, of course," he replied. "Don't you remember that he used to come to play cricket with us?"

"With us?"

"The East Boldon cricket team." I hadn't known that. My cousin is ten years older than me.

"So ... what was he like?"

"In what way?"

"Well, wasn't he the most famous man in County Durham in those days?"

"Well I suppose so, but he just came to have a game on odd Saturdays"

"So what was he like?"

"Just a nice man to be around... good sense of humour ...no airs and graces."

Another Sunderland fan told a typical story (on the Readytogo.net website) about Shack when he was older. "My two sons looked his phone number up when he was living in the Lake District and rang him up. He spoke to them for about 20 minutes. They were 8 and 11. They hung up before I came back, but what a gentleman."

He was above all a family man. He was married for almost sixty years, often travelled with his wife and was proud that his three sons had careers in the professions (as a lawyer, a doctor and a chartered surveyor). Towards the end of Shack's life one of his sons recalled that his father, although not a perfect parent (who was? ... there were fewer in those days of more distant fathers) was thoughtful, intelligent, highly reasonable and humorous.

Perhaps the best guide to how Shack saw himself is in the foreword to his book, which was written by Sunderland's manager, Bill Murray. It was particularly surprising that Shack should have asked for Murray to write it as Murray was being vociferously critical of him at the time, towards the end of his career (he was hiding a ruined ankle). In the foreword to Shack's book Bill Murray called him ...

> "An artist who *cares little for praise and damnation* (Murray's italics), and how it had let him down on occasions. He is a player who seems prompted by an imp of mischief ... With all his ability, his wonderful ball control, he could have been a truly great player, if that imp of mischief had let him play straightforward football; but then he would have been an orthodox player, and orthodoxy is far removed from his makeup."

Shack probably relished the phrase "cares little for praise or damnation". But it is unlikely that it was true. He cared a lot about how he (or his devil) played the game and also about how the game needed to change.

16

His Footballing Twin in Brazil

Shack was a one-off, at least in England. But six thousand miles away there was another player whose close ball control was even better. It was the Brazilian winger, Garrincha, whose glittering shooting star lit up the greatest years of Brazilian football, before collapsing into a black hole of disturbing sadness.

His fate gave a little foretaste, around the time that the English players were breaking free of tight controls, of how allowing a footballer uncontrolled fame and riches at an early age could lead to ruin.

Garrincha was born eleven years after Shack, but died much earlier, at 49.

While the rest of the world regards Pele as the greatest Brazilian footballer, his fellow countrymen loved Garrincha more.

He and Shack were different in many ways, but there were also great similarities.

First, they were both very small when young. Shack was the smallest player on the pitch when he first played for England Boys, and Manuel Francisco dos Santos (his real name) was so small that his sister Rosa called him Garrincha, the local name for a little wren - and the nickname stuck.

The name suited him, because he was a simple child, without ambition. He didn't even take football seriously. When Brazil lost the World Cup on their home turf in 1950, he had gone fishing rather than listening to the final on the radio. It was only reluctantly that he went for trials at the big Rio de Janeiro clubs and at one of them he was told to go home because he had not brought any boots. But by then he was already a prodigy. He had started work at the age of 14 at a local textile factory and was sacked for laziness, but he was brought back because the boss of the factory's football club wanted him in the team.

Secondly, both were gifted with close ball control that singled them out from the rest of their generation. In Garrincha's case his sublime skill seemed little short of miraculous considering his physical abnormalities. While Shack's were limited to very large feet and long toes, Garrincha was born with both legs bent and one leg six centimetres shorter than the other. He also had acute scoliosis, or curvature of the spine: his backbone was like a giant S shape. Both the shortness and deformities have some similarities to those of Messi, who was also very small and had extensive surgery for growth hormone deficiency. (Another sufferer from scoliosis is Usain Bolt).

Unaccountably these deficiencies resulted in the skill described by Eduardo Galeano, in his book, Football in the Sun and Shade:

"When he was out there, the pitch was a circus ring, the ball a tamed animal, the match a party invitation. Garrincha nurtured his pet, the ball, and together they created such mischief that people almost died laughing. He jumped over it, it gamboled around him, hid itself away, skipped off and made him run after it. And on the way, his opponents just ran into each other."

While Shack was the clown prince, Garrincha was 'The Chaplin of football' and 'The Joy of the People'. And, as with Shack, one of Garrincha's fellow players at the 1958 and 1962 World Cup finals, Mario Zagallo, said "Garrincha was too unpredictable, even for us his team-mates."

A third similarity was that both Shack and Garrincha played to entertain as much as to win, revelling in deceiving defenders with their feints and swerves, taunting them as a toreador taunts a bull. Garrincha inspired the first bullfighting chants of "olé" at football grounds. They started during a 1958 club game for Botafogo in which he tortured the River Plate defender Vairo, constantly teasing, feinting and running past him to "olé"s from the crowd. The display ended with

Garrincha leaving the ball behind and sprinting up the pitch with Vairo running after him until Garrincha stopped, pointed to the abandoned ball and beat Vario back to it, the chants of olé exploding into laughter.

A fourth similarity was that their mischievousness could irritate the national team selectors.

In 1954 Garrincha was already playing exceptionally, but Brazil had other talented players in his position - notably Julio - and with the selectors turning to the European style of play based on teamwork, Garrincha was not named in the squad for the 1954 World Cup. Then a month before the 1958 finals Garrincha blotted his copy book again in a club match by beating four defenders and the goalkeeper, and then, rather than putting it into the empty net, waiting for another defender to run back. Garrincha then dribbled past him again before scoring. Despite the demonstration of sublime skill the coaches considered it irresponsible and dropped him for Brazil's first two matches of the 1958 World Cup

He did, however, play in the next two games, and this marked the beginning of Brazilian football's golden partnership. With Pele and Garrincha playing together, the national team never lost a match. (Pele's goal scoring record was extraordinary: in 1961 he scored 111 goals in 75 appearances.) But newspapers reported that Pelé and Garrincha were only picked after a rebellion by the players. It was denied by the players afterwards, but it is nevertheless remembered. Whatever the truth, this was the centre of a team that became the greatest in Brazilian history; and Brazil have remained the favourites in most of World Cups since then - even in 2014 World Cup, the scene of their humiliating 7-1 defeat by Germany.

The Brazilian style - in which individual skills are favoured over team tactics and where dribbles and flicks are preferred over physical challenges or long passes - was cemented during the 1958 and 1962 World Cups, came to its peak in 1970 and has never really faded. There are still more Brazilians playing in the top leagues abroad than any other nationalities.

This was not always the case. Before Garrincha, Pele and the rest of the Brazilian team arrived at the 1958 World Cup in Sweden, Brazil were considered second-rate even on their own continent. Uruguay was the dominant Latin team, having won the first World Cup in 1930 and then, embarrassingly for Brazil, beating the hosts in 1950 to claim their second crown (Italy was the only other winner in these years). The defeat in 1950 on their own ground was remembered as 'The Fateful Final'. It had left such deep scars on the Brazilians that they went to Sweden accompanied by a psychologist, a move almost unheard of at the time. It may have been successful, as Brazil won three of the next four World Cups, and Garrincha played in two. He helped Brazil win the cup in 1958 and then hit the pinnacle of his fame when he was voted player of the 1962 World Cup tournament after a series of superb performances and four goals, which made him the tournament's joint top scorer.

"What planet is Garrincha from?" asked Chile's Mercurio newspaper after Brazil had eliminated the hosts in the 1962 semi-final. After Brazil went on to win a second World Cup in succession, many people worldwide considered him the second greatest player in his country's history, after Pele.

He went on to play 50 international matches for Brazil between 1955 and 1966, and was a starter for the national team in the 1958, 1962 and 1966 World Cups. Brazil only lost one match with him on the pitch, against Hungary at the 1966 World Cup. He also won three Rio State Championships with Botafogo, and was named in the World Team of the 20th Century chosen in 1998 for the opening ceremonies of the 1998 World Cup in Paris by a panel of 250 international football journalists. (The team was Yashin, Carlo Alberto Torres, Beckenbauer, Moore, Nilton Santos, Cruyff, di Stefano, Garrincha, Platini, Maradona and Pele.)

The response of one British newspaper to Garrincha's performance against England in the 1962 World Cup – which Brazil won 3–1 and advanced to the semi-finals – was that he "was Stanley Matthews, Tom Finney and a snake charmer all rolled into one".

But only four years after this, when the World Cup came around again in 1966, he was a pale shadow of the old player. A long-term knee injury had slowed the electric bursts of speed that had once made him so unstoppable. Garrincha's deformed legs had been his strength. But now they were his weakness. The way his tibia met his femur meant that each time he swivelled his body the cartilage was crushed, a problem compounded by the violence of football tackles. His last game in a Brazil shirt was their 3-1 defeat by Hungary in 1966 - the first time he had ever been on the losing side for his country in his 60th appearance.

By now financial problems were building up. Unlike Shack, he was not the brightest, unable to write and therefore unable to sign a contract when he became a professional. In psychometric tests he was classed as below primary school age. Even on the pitch his appreciation of what was going on could be only partial. In the final against Sweden it was said that Garrincha didn't even know who the opponents were, and at the finish he meandered around the pitch asking "is it the end?"

Meanwhile, having reached the pinnacle of his success as the player of the World Cup, Garrincha had been spending money like water on a host of friends, hangers-on, girlfriends and his vast and growing family; and while they revelled in his being a free spirit on the pitch, Garrincha's friends started to worry about his innocence off it. They suggested that he should employ a financial adviser, and two bank representatives went to his home in Pau Grande. They were shocked to discover money rotting in cupboards, behind furniture and in fruit bowls. His house was a slum. His club, Botafogo, had taken advantage of

Garrincha's naivety. They gave him blank contracts to sign, and then filled them in with salaries as low as they could get away with. Garrincha was the club's main selling-point, yet he did not earn as much as his team-mates. But when he complained, the fans turned against him, accusing him of being mercenary. After the World Cup up in 1962 his second wife, a well-known singer who had negotiated many contracts herself, got him more organised. But by the time he got a fair contract he had arthrosis in both legs and could not play and the club docked half of his salary. He had an operation but recovered only partially and was sold to Corinthians in 1966.

By the end of the 1960s, Garrincha's career was more or less over, although he spent years drifting around both South America and Europe trying to prolong it. He needed money to support his alcoholism and his now vast family, but he also needed to work because it was the only way he could stop drinking. In 1968 he signed for Colombian team Atlético Junior and in the same year he went back to Brazil and joined Flamengo, where he would stay until 1969. In 1971, there were rumours that he would join French club Red Star FC 93, but he never signed and returned to Brazil.

Unfortunately he never played in European leagues, despite being targeted by rich European clubs like Juventus who tried to sign him in 1954. Real Madrid of Spain also tried to sign him in 1959 after some stunning performances on a tour of Europe. And AC Milan and Juventus considered jointly signing him in 1963 (he would have to spend a season with each); a deal that would have been unique in football.

A few years later with neither income nor savings, Garrincha asked the Brazilian Sports Confederation for a loan to buy a house. He was refused. On the same day, he disappeared and was found drunk and crying in front of a church in Rio's city centre.

* * *

When it comes to differences between Garrincha and Shack, one of the greatest was that Garrincha's mischievousness and playing to the crowd did not prevent his winning fifty caps for his country, scoring twelve goals as winger and scoring five times in his dozen World Cup finals matches. It was an extraordinary achievement considering his torrid, complicated and generally disastrous private life.

Unlike Shack, Garrincha was a heavy drinker, going through a bottle of local rum (cachaca) a day, reportedly before games in some cases. Throughout his career he astounded colleagues with his capacity for alcohol. At first it did not affect his play, but problems started when he was 25. In particular, after playing well in the World Cup in 1958, Garrincha put on weight because of his drinking, and he was dropped from the national team for a friendly match in Rio against England in 1959. But he was soon back in the team and may have been the best player in the world over the next three or four years. It was only in the mid-1960s that the alcohol really took its toll, and when he retired the drinking increased.

Legend has it that he lost his virginity to goat, but then women came into his life, and he went on to have at least fourteen children.

He had eight daughters with his first wife, Nair Marques, who was his childhood sweetheart. She was a factory worker from his home town of Pau Grande. They married in 1952 and separated in 1965. But during their time together he had affairs with many women including an actress who was the Brazilian vice-president's ex-lover; a mistress called Iraci who announced her first pregnancy on the day his wife, Nair, gave birth to their fifth child; a showgirl called Angelita Martinez; and a famous singer. In 1959 he went on tour with Botafogo in Sweden and made a local girl pregnant.

He eventually left his wife for the famous singer. They met on the day Brazil won the World Cup. As the naked players celebrated in the dressing room, Elza Soares, an alluring samba singer, walked in and embraced Garrincha in the shower. It was the beginning of a stormy affair that lasted for more than fifteen years. They were the country's top celebrities in the country's favourite entertainments - football and samba – and they had similar humble backgrounds. They set up house in Rio, leaving Garrincha's wife and growing family back in Pau Grande. This turned many Brazilians against him, and when he went on to marry Soares, who had also been married before, in an unofficial ceremony in 1966, the Brazilian press did not approve.

By the time of the marriage Garrincha's career was already fading and his drinking worsened. He became suicidal at times and Elza thought that a change of scene might pull him out of it. They moved to Rome, but while Elza found work as a singer Garrincha had little to do except drink. Eventually he was made "coffee ambassador" for the Brazilian Coffee Institute. It was undemanding work: all he needed to do was turn up at European trade fairs and shake hands at the Brazilian stall. He failed spectacularly. On their return to Brazil, Elza had an idea to stop Garrincha drinking: they would have a child. And so Manuel Garrincha dos Santos Junior - Garrincha, Little Garrincha - was born in 1976. But with a baby in the house, it got worse. Garrincha started attacking Elza, and after he hit her in a drunken rage she moved out, fearing that he would turn his violence on to the child. After fifteen years together, their relationship ended. She was heartbroken by the breakup, but later, in her seventies, she is still singing, and recently married a handsome man forty five years younger than herself.

Like footballers today Garrincha liked cars, and he drove them badly. In 1959, returning from a tour, he drove home to Pau Grande and ran over his father, Amaro. He drove off without stopping, with an enraged mob chasing after him, and when they caught up with him they found him "drunk, almost catatonic, and with no grasp of what he had done."[1] His father died soon afterwards of liver cancer after a life of alcoholism. Then in the 1960s he had an accident with Elza that knocked some of her teeth out. But worst of all, after driving up to Pau Grande with Elza's mother to see his children, he hit a lorry at 50mph on the way back. The car turned over and Elza's mother died. The accident triggered a depression. He tried to gas himself - one of the first of several suicide attempts. These events only accelerated his drinking.

His end when it came was extraordinarily sad. He had played on after drink had ruined him physically and mentally, but was finally forced to give up at the age of 39.

Seven years later he was invited to star at the annual Rio Carnival. It was reported that they sat him on a float and drove him through the city for the cheering crowd to see him again. But, slumped like a dead body, he was oblivious to it all - numbed by DTs and medication, and hemorrhaging, as the whole of Rio watched horrified from the roadside and on television. Pele, sitting in a VIP box, threw him down a garland. Garrincha didn't even notice. The cameras covering the procession cut back to Pele who was now shaking his head and muttering "Oh, my God" at the wreckage of his old friend.

He had been living in an old house built for workers in a textile mill.

Three years later he died, destitute and alone, aged 49. The doctors had not recognised him when he came into the hospital. His body was bloated, poisoned by alcohol and unrecognisable from the agile athlete he had once been, and he was transferred to a psychiatric hospital in an alcoholic coma. He died at 6am the following morning.

And so one of the most adored Brazilians of all time passed away, a ruined lonely pauper. It was just twenty years after he was widely recognised to be the greatest footballer on earth, in a country where football was everything and his photograph was in every newspaper, that Garrincha died of cirrhosis of the liver, attached to a drip in a Rio hospital, after a three day bender in a bar.

In the cemetery where Garrincha is buried there is a small memorial expressing Brazil's love for the two-time world champion. It reads: "He was a sweet child; he spoke with the birds." It was hardly an accurate epitaph - except in one sense, that the childlike 'little wren' would have been happier had he been protected, like the English players of the time, from the temptations that came with untold fame and riches.

17

His Later Years

Didier Drogba, the formidable Ivory Coast and ex-Chelsea striker looks more like an African warrior, but he is in fact a qualified chartered accountant. He studied the subject at a French university early in his football career, to have a fall-back position if he failed to make the grade, or to take care of his future when he finished. And many continental players were encouraged by their clubs to take similar precautions.

English clubs, however, have never done much to encourage their players to plan for their lives post football. In fact self-improvement could sometimes backfire. Even comparatively recently, in the 1990s, a hard tackling Chelsea full back who made the mistake of reading the Guardian in the changing room, and was overheard recommending an exhibition at the Tate Gallery to a multilingual Danish player, was taunted on the pitch as being gay. Graeme le Saux was in fact heterosexual and married with two children. His other offence may have been having gone to university, which could have been seen as rather uppity in the dressing room.

But it was even worse in the 1950s. Most players left school in their mid-teens and joined a club almost immediately; and as Shack recalled, the typical footballer left the game at "the average retiring age of 35, in the prime of life, jobless, with only a few hundred pounds from the benevolent fund, not trained for a trade or profession, and homeless … eviction from club houses is automatic when clubs decide to dispense with their players' services." Not surprisingly, many footballers fell on hard times.

Shack, however, was more farsighted. While he was still playing he had set up small shops - hairdressers, sweetshops, ice cream shops – with his modest savings and even mischievously told Sunderland that he was considering retiring in 1950 to look after them. Also, he could still play some professional cricket after he left Sunderland. But that was not enough for him. He needed a more substantial job, preferably connected with football which had been his life. Management had no attraction for him; in 1955 he had written "I have often been asked if I would fancy going in for the managerial side of soccer when my playing days are over. The prospect appals me. I can think of no more precarious occupation, no quicker method of ruining my health." But what he did have was a flair for words. He was known for his sharp wit and he now had a successful book behind him.

Shack at 35

And so he became a journalist, as a football and sports reporter for the Daily Express for the next six years, and then for the Sunday People for the following twenty years. It kept him in touch with the game he loved and old friends, and it did not tax him too much. He was once overheard chatting to Jackie Milburn in the Roker press box about the state of the economy in the late 1970s, around the time that the UK had to be bailed out by the IMF, just before the winter of discontent.

"Len," said Jackie, "they say that if this carries on we could have the return of the 3-day week."

"Sod that, Jackie," Shack replied, "I'm not working an extra day for anyone!"

He claimed never to have been too serious about anything – that he had played football not for money, celebrity or adulation but for the pleasure of being paid to keep fit.

But his editor, Neville Holtham, who had idolised Shack when he was a player, would say that he was proud to have him on his own team of match reporters in later years

His reports from the start echoed the way he had played football, full of laconic playful cameos. For example:

"I do know about a worse defence then Leyton Orient's – but the chap being defended was hanged. That's nothing to do with football, I know. So what? Neither had this Orient rear-guard" (April 6 1959)

"If all the top-line managers are not queuing up to sign Grimsby Town's Ralph Hunt in the next few weeks then I'm a Chinaman ... Hunt rocked solid Colchester in the 59th minute with a header that out-Lawtoned the fabulous Tommy. And eight minutes later he tore up the field like a gazelle, collared a Jimmy Fell pass and clattered home a shot from 16 yards" (Sept 2 1959)

"If you like your soccer rough and tough then Borough Park, Workington, was your place last night. Workington, after being two goals up at half time and then letting the game slip away from them, should be put on bread and water... after that, with Aldershot playing the army game – bash, bash, bash – Workington should have had an easy win" (Sept 11 1959)

"Timber! Freddie Truman is splintering those stumps again." (He covered cricket as well as football)" May 11 1962

"They played Yuri Gagarin football - boot the ball in the air and rush after it." April 21 1961

He could be sarcastic, even about Sunderland. Writing about their first game in the Second Division, exactly a year after his damaged ankle stopped him playing, he began his match report, "Sunderland started with a bang. Like a puncture." This, however, may have reflected his dislike for the new iron disciplinarian manager, Alan Brown, whose first season in charge had seen Sunderland relegated to the Second Division for the first time (while Shack, in contrast, had kept them up from 1948, when he came on board to save them from relegation, to the 1957/58 season at the beginning of which his ankle collapsed).

He retired from journalism when he was sixty one and moved from his beloved north east to Cumbria, where his wife's sister lived. There he still played golf and partnered the sister-in-law and her husband in small businesses - flats for rent, a café etc. But when his health deteriorated he sold some of them and bought a holiday home in Tenerife to spend the winters in a warmer climate.

By then he had mild emphysema, after a lifetime of smoking, five years working in the mines, and much of his life living in the industrial north east, with its the blackened buildings, smog and icy winds. He was also going deaf.

In 2000 he had a heart attack and died a few months later at the age of seventy eight.

At the end his way with words has not deserted him. A few weeks before his death he confessed to a journalist friend that, unlike before, he was now finding it "awfully hard work doing nothing." He may or may not have been aware that it was a line from Oscar Wilde's 'The Importance of Being Earnest.'

The day he died, a journalist was walking through the centre of Sunderland when he saw a local newspaper billboard announcing the sad news that "Shack is dead". He handed the vendor his coins, but before she took them she said:

"It's not in the paper, pet. It was too late for them. I just thought people would like to know."

* * *

Sixteen years after his death and fifty eight years after he stopped playing his star still burns brightly on Wearside. Sunderland has a very active Senior Supporters Association that holds meetings for the over 55s, with up to a hundred attending, and recently the Sunderland club historian, Rob Mason, organised a poll of the oldest fans, all except one in their eighties, to find their favourite player of all time. It was not a hot topic, as all except one plumped immediately for Shack. They all had their stories. One 76 year old was able to corroborate the story that Shack used to kick the ball against the corner flag at the right angle to beat an opponent. He had seen him do it twice in a game to prove that it was not a fluke, and he had a clear view because he was standing under a floodlit pylon at the Fullwell end. Another in her eighties recalled him racing for goal after his boot came off and still scoring. But despite the unanimity that he had been the best, they were not uncritical. A lady aged 81 was *still* upset that he lost Sunderland a place in a cup final when he failed to make a tackle to stop the opponents from scoring, "but he didn't and I always blamed him for that." Another of the oldies said that he knows people who never went to another game after Shack retired, adding that he met Shack many times when he was young, and that he was a gentleman.

18

The End of the Maximum Wage

It was not until 1957 that the battle for the removal of the maximum wage took off, with the appointment of Jimmy Hill as the new chairman of the Professional Footballers Association (PFA). The PFA records the contrast between Hill, "with his comparative youth and gift of the gab" and "the grumpy old men of the Football League, who, with their cigars, Homberg hats and tendency to talk in riddles, seemed like throwbacks to the inter-war years". Hill was, like Shackleton, a grammar school boy, having won a scholarship to Henry Thornton's, in the London suburb of Clapham, where he excelled at cricket (football being discouraged) before he went on to play football for Fulham. Tough talking and articulate, with the air of a barrack room lawyer at times, he fostered a new air of militancy amongst the players. In the years immediately after the misery of the Second World War, the players would probably have accepted their lot with working class docility. In many ways life would have been good for a footballer. But militancy was on the rise.

Hill and the players faced formidable and deeply conservative opposition in the form of the Football League, and especially in the person of its Secretary, Alan Hardaker. A bleak faced ex-Naval Officer, he was notorious for his xenophobic, insular attitudes and splenetic outbursts, memorably telling a Times journalist that European football was full of "too many wogs and dagoes". The comment was made in support of his boycott of Chelsea's attempt to be the first English team to enter the European Cup competition in 1955 after they won the English Championship. The Times journalist went on to write that "Hardaker, Football League Secretary and unbending autocrat, once told me that he didn't like dealing with football in Europe ... His attitude was supremely negative and self-aggrandizing, probably influenced by the fear that his own competition (Hardaker had introduced the League Cup) would be overshadowed by the new one." Hardaker had made the peculiar claim that "The FA Cup is football's Ascot, the League Cup its equivalent of Derby Day at Epsom" – a distinction that would have mystified most football supporters. He later went on to defend the player's contract that Shack had called the 'evil document', arguing in the High Court for no change (on behalf of the League Management Committee, reflecting the views of the clubs' directors who had instructed him on how to proceed).

In 1969, he was reported to have commented, when asked about the proposal that retired payers should sit on disciplinary committees, that "I wouldn't hang a dog on the evidence of people like that." It was a notable example of the middle stairs-downstairs class divide in professional football (see Chapter 7). Another lack of foresight was his blocking of attempts by television companies to show football matches live in 1955, 1956 and 1967, and later he offered the opinion in his autobiography that "regular live football would undermine the game's health". He even resisted the broadcasting of football highlights on television, initially rejecting a three-year deal in 1973, worth £750,000, although the offer was finally accepted after long negotiations.

But despite his views on wogs, dagoes, players, dogs and, it seemed, *any* modern developments - or maybe because of them - Hardaker enjoyed the full confidence of the Football League's Management Committee, which in practice delegated many of its powers to him to act independently. In his autobiography, he admitted that, with this level of autonomy, he was perceived as "arrogant and high-handed" and had "frequently been called a dictator" by club officials.

The League's president, Joe Richards, was equally conservative. He was an England team selector out of the mould despised by Shack. He had broken a leg badly when he was young and had never played football himself but he had climbed the ladder into a position of authority by joining the Football League management committee and the FA Council. A blunt cigar-smoking whisky-drinking northern businessman, he was short of stature and had a moustache. He had a chauffeur for his Rolls Royce and called meetings in the Café Royal in London. At the end of the Second World War he had been the manager of his town's largest coal mine, and was also a freemason, a conservative councillor and Chairman of Barnsley football club. He was 69 when he was elected president of the football league in 1957. Like Hardaker, Richards was authoritarian in manner, a straight talking Yorkshireman, but not particularly articulate. And now he had to face the first generation of grammar school boys representing the players.

In 1959, in a landmark event on TV, Richards represented the Football League in a debate with Jimmy Hill and Danny Blanchflower, the fluent Northern Irish captain of Tottenham Hotspur, over whether the treatment of footballers could reasonably be compared with that of serfs. This had been Shack's expression for the standard contract that prohibited players from changing clubs.

Danny Blanchflower was no stranger to Richards, because Richards had been the chairman at Blanchflower's first English club, Barnsley; and while he was there Blanchflower had personal experience of the demeaning way in which footballers were transferred without their knowledge or agreement. The story is similar to Shack's when he was transferred from Bradford to Newcastle United in 1946 (see Chapter 7). In Blanchflower's case he had asked for a transfer in 1951. But although his request was accepted the club told him there were no offers. Finding this difficult to believe he asked an old college friend who worked on the local telephone exchange to do some eavesdropping, and discovered that there had in fact been enquiries. The club, however, continued to deny it, until one day the Richards told him to be ready to travel next morning.

The Chairman didn't tell Blanchflower where they were going, but on the journey he interrogated him about his background, his family and his education. When they arrived at their destination, his biographer[9] records that Blanchflower's only surprise was "that he wasn't led into the hotel where the deal was done in chains with a lead around his neck". He was taken down to the kitchens of the hotel to be given something to eat, while Richards disappeared to deal with the mystery club in a proper dining room. Then, the deal done, he returned to tell Danny that he had arranged to transfer him to Aston Villa and that he should now meet their chairman and team manager. Richards assured Danny that he had given him a good character reference. Danny's reaction was outrage at the notion that his character was somehow in the gift of the chairman. There was no suggestion that the player might want to make up his own mind. He was to move on the same terms as he had at Barnsley - necessarily so, because the maximum wage was the same at both clubs.

By the time of the TV debate, however, Danny was, at 33, a fluent speaker and a deep thinker who knew his own mind and was said to dominate any room he entered. Some years later when asked before a match on TV "Who do you think will win?", he replied "I don't know: that's why they're playing the match." He was also highly self-confident, being the only person to have walked off the set of Eamonn Andrews's much-loved TV show This is Your Life, saying that it was an invasion of his privacy.

Not surprisingly, Hill and Blanchflower were seen to have won the debate.

A year later the players' union was on the brink of a breakthrough on the maximum wage and the players' contracts.

* * *

It was the vehicle favoured by Shack – the threat of a national strike - that finally brought about the reforms. Towards the end of his career Shack had alienated some of his fellow players by refusing to sign a document confessing that he was one of the many players who had received under the counter payments.

---

[9] Danny Blanchflower: A Biography of a Visionary, by Dave Bowler

This was a gambit conceived by Jimmy Hill in the early days of his chairmanship of the PFA, designed to force the League into recognizing the damaging effects of the maximum wage. But Shack thought it was too indirect an approach to the archaic control of wages when compared with a strike.

The end game in the battle for free wages was described in detail in Gary Imlach's "My Father and other Working Class Heroes." It is an extraordinary tale of stubborn resistance by the clubs to fair treatment of their players.

The story is taken up in 1960 when Hill and the Professional Footballers' Association had reached the stage of applying to the Ministry of Labour to force a response from the unbending Football League on reforms. For three months the League had been monitoring a nationwide sounding of opinion. It had started in the clubs, where votes were taken for and against strikes. Imlach recalls how at his father's club, Luton, the chairman refused to accept a vote in favour of the strike and summoned the players to the boardroom. There he demanded a show of hands in front of their masters. When all except three raised their hands in favour of the strike the chairman responded by telling them "I hope you know what you are doing, you are going to be out of a job." Their spokesman asked if he was trying to frighten them, to which the chairman replied "No but it just won't happen, you are fighting a lost cause."

The votes at the clubs were followed by mass meetings in the regions. The first was held in London where players from the south of England were overwhelmingly in favour of striking. Fearing that the Midlands would go the same way, the Coventry City chairman was reported to have argued "I gather the impression that the majority of players at yesterday's meeting did not want to strike, but were swayed by one man. It may suit that one man to have a strike but the vast majority of footballers know that a strike is not in the best interests of themselves or their clubs." The man he was referring to was Jimmy Hill, and the Coventry City chairman had seen the way Hill had galvanized the players into a new attitude of militancy. He could see the writing on the wall.

At another of the meetings, in the north, a key turning point came after a Bury player called Andrew Jackson spoke up against the strike. His argument was that £20 a week was a good wage for an open air life when compared with the £10 a week his father earned for eight hour shifts in a Derbyshire coal mine. He was silenced by a Bolton Wanderers full back who replied "Yes, I know your dad. And you can tell him that I could do his job but he couldn't do mine, week in week out, which sometime means marking brother Matthews here."

As he spoke he was standing beside Stanley Matthews, who had personal experience of the football establishment's assumption of divine right to authority over the national game, when he was reprimanded by the Football Association for playing in a charity 'Tennis Stars versus Showbiz Eleven' football match with his son, who was a professional tennis player. This broke an FA rule that "their" players were not allowed to play with or against unaffiliated clubs. The FA official was able to report back that Matthews had given a written assurance that it would not happen again. And now the great man, still playing at forty-six years of age, gave his support to strike action.

When the meeting ended Gordon Taylor, a future chairman of the PFA, recalled that the vote was 254 votes to 6 in favour of the strike. Roger Hunt, who later played in the 1966 World Cup Final, reported that Liverpool had allowed their players to attend the meeting on condition that they voted against the strike. But when they saw the others raise their hands, they followed along with everyone else.

Hill followed up meetings with four demands, submitted to the League and to the Ministry of Labour for information, in April 1960. They were:

- The end of the maximum wage
- Reform of the player's contract
- A new retaining system, meaning the ending of the clubs' ownership of their players
- Players to get a share of a transfer fee

The League took five months to reply, and when they did they ignored all the demands, offering only another £2 on the maximum wage and some minor items.

Another round of mass meetings was called, with more speeches by the union leaders.

With a week to go before the strike the clubs were so desperate that they tried to bring the next Saturday's fixtures, which were due to be hit by the strike, back to the Friday, in order to extract one last day of income. They sent telegrams to all the clubs in England instructing them to reschedule all their games to Friday evening, or afternoon for clubs without floodlights. Players who refused to turn out would be considered to have broken their contracts. This provoked a rapid series of moves and counter-moves. The players responded to the League's moving the fixtures back by a day by stating that they would start the strike a day earlier; and the Football League responded by stating that the games would go ahead using replacement players. The TUC then called on its members to boycott blackleg games, and the Professional Footballers Association considered introducing their own league. The clubs hinted that players might be evicted from their club houses.

Three days before the strike was due to start the Ministry of Labour called for last ditch talks.

Joe Richards, president of the Football League responded: "I will be at the meeting if my presence means avoiding a strike but I am not going to waste my time. I am not budging on the transfer system, which must remain as long as there is a league competition in the country."

But Richards did attend the meeting, which took place on January 18th 1961 at the Ministry of Labour. Later, Hill was to ask "Wasn't it Queen Mary Tudor who had 'Calais 1558' written on her heart? Well, when they finally open me up, they'll find 'Ministry of Labour, January 18, 1961' carved on mine."[10]

---

[10] http://www.theguardian.com/football/2001/jan/15/newsstory.sport1

Those present on the footballers' side were Hill, Cliff Lloyd (the PFA's secretary and Hill's deputy), George Davies (the union's solicitor), with the Football League represented by Richards, Hardaker and Joe Mears, the chairman of Chelsea football Club. The referee was a representative from the Ministry of Labour, possibly aware that government was fearful of having an electorate with no pools coupons to be filled in if the strike went ahead.

Hill commented on the atmosphere at the meeting: "League football had been set in its feudal time warp. January the 18th was the watershed, but even in their shell shock the league and its chairmen looked to overturn the agreement. They had spent generations looking down their noses at players and now, even at that meeting at the ministry, they presumed to treat us as inferior beings. Being totally in charge of us was ingrained into their culture. And to find me, not a venerable ex-player but a lad who was still actually playing for a club they controlled, must have been anathema to them."

The Football League, however, caved in, conceding both the end of the maximum wage and the players' contract. Afterwards, the Ministry of Labour announced it at a press conference of sixty journalists.

Victory at last.

Or so it seemed. Until the individual clubs tried to torpedo what had been agreed.

The clubs' chairmen arranged an extraordinary general meeting to vote on formal approval of the proposed reforms and when it emerged that the consensus remained deeply hostile to the contractual reforms they decided not to ratify the agreement announced by the Ministry of Labour. They deleted the contractual reforms from the motion, limiting the vote to the ending of the maximum wage. They preferred this concession to the ending of their precious quasi-feudal control over "their" players.

At the meeting Joe Richards acted as if the League's decision had never happened. "Come what may," he said "we intend to keep the retain and transfer system"; and as reported in the Guardian, "the distraught league management committee and its reactionary and apoplectic club chairmen spent the following months prevaricating and repatching the agreement, hedging their bets and going back on their word."

But Shack, now a football journalist with a network of contacts, was already working behind the scenes to get the hated 'players contract' challenged in the courts – by introducing a victim of the system to a sympathetic businesnman will to back his case financially.

[It took another two years before the clubs' ownership of their players was eventually loosened. This time it was decided in the courts after a discontented star at Newcastle United, George Eastham, was told that he could not leave to join Arsenal. Eastham took United to the highest court in England, won his case, and the players finally became free to move in 1963. And even then clubs resisted the ruling of the High Court, in which Justice Wilberforce denounced the practices in the memorable sentence "to anyone not hardened to the acceptance of the practice it would seem inhuman and incongruous to the spirit of a national sport." The clubs pored over the many paged wording of the judgment and exploited convenient clauses to their advantage, and it was only after the EU's Bosman ruling in (see Chapter 20) that the old rules were finally swept away.]

There was even a last stand by the clubs to resist the ruling on the ending of the maximum wage as well as the players' contract. Newcastle United refused to pay more, and soon afterwards the club chairmen met at the Café Royal (!) in London to try to hatch up a new unofficial maximum wage. However, the chairman of Fulham, the comedian Tommy Trinder, was instrumental in having the plot aborted.

The rear guard resistance soon faded away. With the floodgates opened, Johnny Haynes, the Fulham and England captain was the first player to be paid £100 a week.

The genie was out of the bottle. But wages did not take off immediately after the abolition of the maximum wage. While Fulham's showbiz chairman appreciated the public relations value of making Johnny Haynes the first £100-a-week player, other clubs, including Manchester United and Liverpool, initially stuck to their wage ceilings. It was only when stars such as Denis Law and Jimmy Greaves left to play in Italy for bigger salaries that the clubs realised they were going to have to pay out more to keep the best players, and by the end of the 1960s, George Best was earning £1,000 a week at Manchester United – a hundred times the top wage at the beginning of the decade.

The trends in (a) top wages and (b) average wages in the 55 years since the abolition of the maximum wage are shown in the following tables.

Highest Premier League Wages 1960-2015

Year	£ a week	Average Increase p.a.
1960	20	...
1970	1,000	48%
1990	10,000	12%
2000	100,000	26%
2010	160,000	5%
2015	300,000	13%

Some landmarks *Wage per week*

1992	Eric Cantona joins Manchester United	£10,000
1996	Alan Shearer joins Newcastle United	£34,000
1999	Roy Keane extends contract at Manchester United	£50,000
2000	Sol Campbell joins Arsenal	£100,000
2005	Steven Gerrard extends contract at Liverpool	£100,000
2006	Shevchenko joined Chelsea	£118,000
2010	Rooney extended contract at Manchester United	£160,000
2011	Sergio Aguero joined Manchester City	£200,000
2014	Rooney, new deal at Manchester United	£300,000

By 2015, the average wage in England's top division was 2,200 times higher than in 1960:-

Average weekly wage in the Top Division of English Football

		Increase p.a.	
		(actual)	(excl. inflation)
1901	£4	..	
1960	£20	3%	
1970	£70	13%	(8%)
1980	£550	23%	(9%)
1990	£1,500	11%	(4%)
2000	£11,000	22%	(18%)
2010	£33,000	12%	(10%)
2015	£44,000	6%	(4%)

Source: Sporting Intelligence and Daily Mail

The main patterns in the average wages and their causes since 1960 were:

o A steady rise of 8% p.a. (in real terms, i.e. after adjusting for inflation) in the 1960s.

o A similar steady rise, at 9% p.a. in real terms during the 1970s. This was far below the nominal increase of 23% p.a. which was mainly attributable to inflation rates that averaged 14% p.a. over the decade mainly because of the increase in the price of oil.

o A lower real rate of increase, at 4% p.a. during the 1980s.

o A massive real increase of 18% p.a. during the 1990s. It had four causes:

First, the founding of the Premier League in 1992, which led to increased incomes for the club to spend. Annual turnstile numbers have risen rose eight million five years before the Premier League started to thirteen million today.

Secondly, the Bosman ruling in 1995 allowed players to move freely at the end of their contracts, or on transfers, to any club in Europe. For example, in 1990 Chelsea had no foreign player on its books, but by 2000 it had 22 - Ed de Goey, Dan Petrescu, Celestine Babayaro, Jes Høgh, Frank Leboeuf, Marcel Desailly, Didier Deschamps, Gustavo Poyet, Mario Melchiot, Roberto Di Matteo, Albert Ferrer, Gabriele Ambrosetti, Tore Andre Flo, Bernard Lambourde, Carlo Cudicini, Samuele Dalla Bona, Gianfranco Zola, Emerson Thome, George Weah (on loan from Milan), Mikael Forssell, Luca Percassi and Gianluca Vialli.

Thirdly, the Bosman ruling also allowed players to ask for higher personal wages, because the new club did not have to pay a transfer fee as well as the wages. Also, the agents encouraged the players to take advantage of this.

Fourthly, new revenues came pouring into clubs from television broadcasts, giving the football clubs more money to spend.

It was against this background that Sol Campbell became the first player to be paid £100,000 a week when he joined Arsenal on one of the new post-Bosman free transfers in 2000, and at the same time the latest television deal had brought football in England almost a billion pounds a year for the first time. This new source of club income was to ensure that the inexorable rise in wages would continue.

In that year David Beckham, who had not yet benefitted from these new developments, was reportedly paid 'only' £28,000 a week, but that was soon to change.

19

The End of the English Footballer's Contract

The footballer's contract that Shack had to sign was a relic of the nineteenth century. As described in Chapter 7 it was the work of a self-appointed group from the top echelons of British society, the newly formed Football Association, whose aims had little in common with what the FA does today. It was set up in heyday of the British empire to codify the rules of football played at private schools, in an era when sport was regarded as a means of developing character and the muscular Christianity idealised by the Victorians. As such it was to be played according to Corinthian principles, ideally by amateurs.

They were opposed to the very idea of professional football, and only turned to the subject of club football after they had dealt with their initial task of codifying rues for amateur and private school teams.

At first they were inclined to outlaw any payments to footballers, and excluded Preston North End from the FA Cup for breaking this rule. Preston admitted that their players were being paid but argued that it was common practice and did not breach regulations. The FA disagreed and expelled them from the competition.

They relented and allowed payment in 1885. But – here is the key point - the conditions of employment were to be strictly regulated. Players had to register with the club they wanted to play for each season, and renew their registration the next year.

Initially the players were free to change clubs at the end of each season, even if their former club wanted to keep them. But in 1893 the rights of the players were squeezed further. Once a player was registered with a Football League club, he could not move to another club, even when the season had finished, without the permission of the club he was registered with. He was effectively a prisoner of the club. Even worse, this rule applied even if the player no longer had a contract with the club holding his registration; that is to say, it had not been renewed after it expired. And, even worse, the club that held his registration was not obliged to play him, or to pay him.

The feudal nature of this setup was compounded by strict regulation of wages. The reason given was that the Football League was becoming more popular and the best players wanted higher wages, and so if a club wished to keep a good player for a new season it often had to offer him a better deal with his new contract. If the player declined the new contract, he could, at least until 1893, sign for another club – say, one that played better football and/or would pay him a higher wage. Some good players who were attracting large crowds were getting £10 a week. At the same time it was feared that more successful teams were going to start to dominate the league because they could to pay higher salaries.

The Football League, which represented the clubs (or at least their managements), also argued that unless wages were capped all the best players would gravitate to the richest clubs - and this should be resisted. A spread of talent over a large number of clubs was considered necessary to sustain the interest of spectators. The patrician overlords probably envisaged a typical small town having a modest football team, a local brass band and a school to teach the mill workers' children to read.

Against this background **Derby County** proposed that the Football League should impose a maximum wage of £4 a week, and in 1900 the **Football Association** passed a rule at its AGM that agreed this figure. It also abolished the payment of bonuses to players.

No limit, however, was imposed on the spiraling transfer fees that were being paid to clubs, as they became aware of the profit they could make by agreeing to release players from their registrations.

Under this system the value of a player was reflected not in wage he was paid but in the transfer fee the club could collect on his disposal. The player earned nothing from his sale except for a minimal signing-on bonus of £10. It was the clubs that made the money, not the players.

In brief, by 1901 the players were owned by the club; they were paid £4 a week; and the clubs could sell them for large sums of which nothing was paid to the players. There was no free market for players to seek wages that reflected their abilities, but a completely free market for clubs to earn transfer fees.

It is extraordinary that such a system was devised in the first place. Even in 1900 there was no similar cap on the wages of electricians or cooks or, more to the point, actors. On the contrary, a famous actor was paid much more than a spear carrier or an extra.

Even more extraordinary were the facts that the players tolerated these rules made by an anachronistic self-appointed nineteenth century body, and that they were still applied sixty years later to players who drew crowds of up to 70,000 and who were the heroes of their towns and cities.

* * *

By the 1950s, however, the FA's system was coming apart at the seams. It was well known that under the counter payments were rife. But it limped on for a few more years with unpleasant results in many cases.

A typical and particularly sad example of the way footballers were treated in the last years before the footballer's contact was abolished was that of Wilf Mannion - a superb ball player, the equivalent of Shack at Middleborough, who played twenty six times for England despite having his career interrupted by the Second World War.

In 1948 Mannion decided that he did not want to renew his yearly contract with Middlesbrough and asked for a transfer. The club manager, David Jack, simply refused him outright, declaring that:

> "Even if a club came to us with a cheque for £50,000 we would not transfer Mannion. Why should we let the best player in Britain go?" (Tom Finney faced a similar

response when an Italian club tried to lure him away from Preston North End.)

Mannion, like all the top players at the time, was paid £12 per week in the playing season and £10 per week in the summer.

However, while on international duty he had learned that some clubs offered under the counter payments – for example, for second jobs that did not really exist or for well-paid part-time jobs. Middlesbrough did not offer such inducements and Mannion wanted to go to a club that did. (He was once approached by the glamorous Italian club Juventus, the club that signed John Charles from Leeds United; Charles spent five years there, earning £25,000 per year, about 35 times what he would have been played in England.)

When David Jack refused to sell him, Mannion went on strike. In response, Middlesbrough refused to pay him, and as a result of his actions the selectors dropped him from the England team that played Northern Ireland in October 1948.

This all became public knowledge and a journalist at the *Sunday People* wrote: "... David Jack, giving the club's side, told me recently: 'If Mannion won't play for us, he will never play in League football again.' Frankly this seems to me to savour of dictatorship." Mannion replied: "The club can put me right out of the game if it wants to. Why, in the name of fairness, must I, or any of my colleagues, be treated like cattle at an auction and be forced to go only where the club desires? I do not hold Middlesbrough entirely responsible. I blame the system which allows such treatment."

Frank Armitage, a businessman who supported Oldham Athletic in the Third Division, tried to help Mannion by offering him a job outside football with his company. Mannion accepted the post and later admitted: "I think he wanted me to join Oldham, but he never said anything specific."

Middlesbrough said they would be willing to transfer him but only at a fee of £30,000 for Mannion. This was much more that Oldham could afford. Mannion then made a statement that: "I will not stand for this rocketing of transfer values. I have considered the matter from all angles and with all its implications and I am stating without reserve that I shall absolutely decline to sign for any club that pays, or even offers to pay, Middlesbrough over £12,000 for me."

Oldham eventually offered £15,000 for Mannion, but Middlesbrough rejected the bid and refused to negotiate. Aston Villa then offered £25,000 and Everton said they were willing to pay £27,000. Tom Whittaker of Arsenal announced he was willing to offer a player-exchange deal.

But David Jack was determined to hold on to Mannion and after a meeting with the Middlesbrough director, Tommy Thomas, the club and Mannion issued a statement: "Middlesbrough Football Club and Wilf Mannion have agreed to sink their differences. It is agreed that there have been faults on both sides. Middlesbrough are delighted to have the player back and he is delighted to return to the scene of his former triumphs."

The dispute had cost Mannion £400 in lost earnings from football. He was also back on the maximum wage of £12 a week but it was assumed that the club had unofficially paid him a large sum of money in order to persuade him to end his strike. David Jack later said that "Mannion now knows that he need have no worry when his playing days are over... The club has already made arrangements to look after him when his playing days are over."

Six years later, when Mannion was coming to end of his career and not always playing, he joined Second Division Hull City for a fee of £4,500; and just before that he told the Sunday People (June, 1954):

> "I would be a wealthy man today if I had listened to even two or three of the black-market propositions put to me during my eighteen years as a player. One offer alone - from a famous first division club - would have put me in clover. It was made to me, unknown to anyone connected with my own club at the time, when I had refused to re-sign for Middleborough. And it took my breath away.

Besides paying my club what would have been a record transfer fee - some £25,000 - these money-is-no-object directors were prepared to hand me £3,000 in ready cash the moment I signed. On top of that I was to get top wages, then £12 a week, as a player; plus a "job" - I put it that way because it was a job in name only as a salesman of something or other - which would have brought me another cool £25 a week. And, just as an incidental, I was to be given £25, to be slipped to me on the railway station, merely for making the trip to talk the offer over."

On joining Hull Mannion remarked "I'm happy to be back in the game again. My urge to play again was so great that I happened to be in the mood when approached by Hull." He also conceded that he was pleased to be playing in the same side as a great friend and fellow rebel, Neil Franklin.

In 1955, however, the Football League asked him for the name of the English club that had tried to bribe him to leave Middlesbrough. They had asked the same of the Welsh international Trevor Ford, and fined him £100 when he admitted it. When Mannion refused he was banned from playing football for life. (Much later he confessed that the club was Aston Villa). The Football League also ordered Middlesbrough not to pay Mannion the benefit money he was due.

J. L. Manning, the sports editor of the *Sunday Dispatch*, made the obvious comment: "It is the directors of the clubs and not this player who should be called to give information under penalty of suspension... The Sunday Dispatch does not want Mannion alone to bear the burden of proof. That is why we made our offer, and repeat it today, that if the League will grant an amnesty to those concerned we will provide them with far more proof than Mannion can. In this way the League could get evidence of the full extent of the racket instead of merely pursuing a single case."

From 1956 onwards Mannion's career was in decline, and after a spell with Cambridge United in the Eastern Counties League he retired in 1958. He then became manager of non-league King's Lynn, but left after one season to run a pub in Stevenage. It was not a success and by 1959 he wanted to get back into football: but no Football League club was interested in taking him on as a manager and in 1960 he joined the production line of the Vauxhall car plant in Luton. Nine months later he became manager of non-league club, Earlestown, but in 1962 the club went bankrupt and Mannion no longer had a job.

Mannion returned to live in Teesside, and enrolled on a Football Association coaching course in 1964. But he could not find a job in football and the following year it was revealed that he had sold his English caps and was living on unemployment benefit.

Another victim of the FA's rules and the ability of club directors to exploit them callously in these last years before the reforms was Frank Brennan, the Newcastle United centre half. The details of how Big Frank's career was ruined by a Newcastle director, after he had dared to set up a sports shops that competed with the director's, can be found in Chapter 7.

* * *

The eventual overturning of the rules governing the archaic player's contract happened two years after the ending of the maximum wage (see last Chapter), and it was enshrined in the results of a court case.

At the time the elements of the terms of footballers' employment had remained largely unchanged since 1893. The rules were that:

1) The player at a club could re-register for the same club at any time between April 1st and the first Saturday in May. Effectively, the contract was thereby renewed.
2) The club could, however, give the player less favourable terms by serving a notice during the month of May giving details of the terms it was offering. Of particular importance here was the rule that *if the Football Association considered the offer to be too low it could refuse the right of the club to*

keep the player, but if it considered the terms reasonable the player could not sign for any other club. Players were allowed to petition the Football Association with their reasons for wanting to move, but if the Association refused to intervene the clubs could retain players indefinitely.

3) The player could be placed on the transfer list at a fee *fixed by the club*.

The Case: Eastham v Newcastle United

The challenge that brought an end to the clubs' ownership of the players came from George Eastham, a Newcastle United inside forward, who declined to sign a new contract in 1959. The reasons for his wanting to leave were straightforward - the inadequate housing with which the club had supplied him (echoing Shack's complaints when he joined Newcastle in 1946), the unsatisfactory secondary job that the club had arranged and their attempts to stop him playing for England's under-23 team. But when he declined a new contract and asked for a transfer the club refused to let him go. He applied twice more and got two more refusals, and a Newcastle United director was reported to have said that he would rather see Eastham shovel coal than play for Arsenal. As Eastham later observed (*Spurling, 2004, Rebels for the Cause*)

> "Our contract could bind us to a club for life. Most people called it the "slavery contract". We had virtually no rights at all. It was often the case that the guy on the terrace not only earned more than us – though there's nothing wrong with that – he had more freedom of movement than us. People in business or teaching were able to hand in their notice and move on. We weren't. That was wrong."

As with Wilf Mannion at Middleborough, Newcastle told Eastham that not only was he forbidden to leave, he would not, in the absence of a new contract, be paid. Most players in the past had, like Wilf Mannion, given up at this point. But Eastham decided to fight.

He discussed the stand-off with Shack who was now a journalist, but well remembered for his crusade against the 'evil document' of the player's contract in his book; and by good fortune Shack was able to introduce him to Ernie Clay, a wealthy businessman and later a director of Fulham football club, who sympathized with the players. Clay, who also turned out to be a wartime friend of Eastham's father, was happy to champion Eastham's cause and to provide financial assistance. Also, he was able to offer George Eastham a job in the meantime, outside football in his cork manufacturing company in Reigate. He then contacted the Professional Footballers Association, asking them to challenge the validity of Eastham's inactive contract with Newcastle United, and to argue that there was a legal flaw in the rules that would not allow a footballer to choose where he was employed. This was a cause that the PFA was happy to follow up, after the Football League had reneged on their agreement at the Ministry of Labour to end the antiquated retain and transfer system in 1961 (see Chapter 18).

The negotiations that followed were tortuous in the extreme. First, the PFA decided to appeal to the Football League against Newcastle's refusal to release Eastham. But the Football League said that this was a domestic matter between club and player. Eastham, his advisors and the PFA then responded that the Football League were failing to apply their own Regulation 19 – stating that any dispute between a player and a club should be settled by the Management Committee of the Football League. The Football League then asked Newcastle to present their case, while at the same time trying to persuade Eastham to re-sign his contract. But without success. The Football League then asked Eastham and his advisers (Clay and the secretary of the PFA) to meet the chairman of Newcastle. But there was still no progress.

At this point Eastham's solicitors sent the Football League the crucial letter. It gave the Football League a third and final chance to adjudicate as their own regulations required. There was no response, and so a writ was issued against Newcastle United, its directors, the Football League and the Football

Association in the Chancery Division of the High Court. Newcastle capitulated by transferring him to Arsenal for £47,000. But Eastham himself received no reply.

Despite having won the transfer he wanted, Eastham nevertheless considered the principle worth fighting for. So with the backing of the PFA (they paid Eastham's legal fees), he took the Newcastle club to the High Court in 1963. In the case, *Eastham v. Newcastle United* Ch. 413, Eastham argued that the FA's regulations constituted an "unfair restraint of trade", and that Newcastle owed him unpaid wages and bonuses.

The case soon became much greater in scope, leading to the submission of vast amounts of evidence covering the history of the Football League since it started in 1888. Then in court the League trotted out all the standard tired arguments that they had used since the nineteenth century, claiming that the end of the retain and transfer system would undermine competition, allow the big clubs to take all the best players, and leave the smaller clubs vulnerable to increasing inequality.

Hardaker continued to believe that he had a conclusive case in favour of the status quo with his extraordinary reference to "the chaotic conditions that had existed before the League was formed " (in 1888!), as if the world not moved on since then.

But the Union's solicitor, Cliff Lloyd, presented a persuasive rebuttal, elaborating on the abominable behaviour of club managements towards "their" players over sixty years, drawing on many cases; and at the end of the trial he was complimented by the judge as being 'a witness who seemed to me much more in touch with the realities of professional football ... than any other witness'.

The rights and wrongs of the case were sometimes difficult to follow because the meanings of some of the key phrases would not have been readily understood by a layman.

Firstly, the precise meaning of the "Retain and Transfer" system that Eastham wanted abolished was not self-evident. In fact, the word "retain" in this context meant the ability of the club to offer a new contract every year. More precisely it meant that by the closing day of each season clubs had to send two lists to the league - the retain list of players they wanted to retain, and the transfer list of players they wanted to transfer. It was, however, a one sided arrangement, because if the player refused the new contract he could not leave; and, even worse, he would not be paid.

The second key phrase that was misleading to a layman was "Restraint of Trade", which was the basis on which Eastham's lawyers attacked the players' contract. To an outsider it would suggest quotas, import tariffs, obstacles to fair competition. But what it actually meant in this case was the freedom or right of a player to seek new employment.

The third important word, "transfer", was used in a way that would be comprehensible to all. But the judge, who seemed well-briefed on most areas of football, did not appear to understand two important points. First, he stated that players could not be transferred without their consent. This was misleading as several top players were not told the names of their new owners until the deal was done - including Shack, Danny Blanchflower and Stewart Imlach (see pages 86-87) Admittedly they could technically have refused but would have found life very difficult at their current clubs if they did. Also, players' requests for transfers were often refused.

Another misapprehension of the judge was his belief that the receipt of a transfer fee was justifiable mainly to enable the club to survive or improve its facilities, while in practice they would usually be seeking to recoup part of the fee they paid to get the player earlier.

The players were, however, fortunate in the judge selected to hear the case. He was Richard Wilberforce, a man noted for his courtesy and good humour. He was a great-great-grandson of the famous anti-slavery reformer William Wilberforce, and highly intelligent, a Fellow of All Souls, Oxford. An obituary recalled that behind the diffident facade lay an extremely kind and modest man who, despite the calibre of his mind, was no blind worshipper of intellect. When puzzled by a case he would often ask his children what they thought, "mentioning no names of course".

Key Points Raised in the Hearing

The key points raised in the course of the hearing are summarised in the following pages (with comments in italics and emphasis in bold type).
    The detail shown here may seem greater than will be digestible by some readers but it is included because it illustrates the point that despite the undoubted intelligence of the judge he did not always grasp the essentials of the players' contract, and the crucial verdict in the players' favour may have owed as much to his heart being in the right place as to the logic of his arguments.

*

Eastham's Attempt to Leave Newcastle
Extracts from The Weekly Law Report, October 18 1963, describe the following steps of Eastham's attempt to leave Newcastle United:

On December 11, 1959 the plaintiff (Eastham) requested in writing to be put on the transfer list.

No formal answer was given, but in conversation the chairman reassured him about finding him a job and having work done on his house.

On April 29 1960 Newcastle United notified him that they had decided to retain him for 1960-1 at his current wage.

He did not re-sign.

On June 28 he was told that he had been retained under the association's rule 26 b.

On June 25 he made a **further** application to be put on the transfer list.

He was interviewed and his conduct was criticised by the manager, Mitten, to whom, on June 27, a newspaper attributed the words **"As far as I am concerned, Eastham won't be transferred.** The board met on Wednesday to consider his application, but I have spoken to the chairman and he feels the same way as I do. **If he wants to play football it will be at Newcastle".**

On June 29 the board rejected the plaintiff's application and he was so informed.

On July 4 he left Newcastle to work for a company in Surrey.

On July 14 he applied under rule 62e to the League's management committee on the grounds that he was unable to arrange his transfer with his club… asking for leave to transfer.

On July 21 Newcastle United sent written observations on the plaintiff's appeal to the League, saying that he had been retained in strict observance of the regulations, and expressing "the sincere hope of the directors that the management committee will uphold them in the stand which they felt bound to take".

On July 28 the management committee considered the appeal and decided that "the matter was entirely between the club and the player".

On July 30 the plaintiff appealed to the league's management committee under rule 19. *(There was no response.)*

On September 28 he again asked the League to deal with his appeal.

Meanwhile no communication whatever had passed from Newcastle United to the plaintiff; nor was there any communication with him at all from the time he left Newcastle.

The Press, however, were carrying frequent statements, said to have been made by the chairman and secretary, to the effect that Newcastle United would not give way, would insist on the plaintiff re-signing, and would not transfer him. The chairman denied almost all the observations attributed to him.

The plaintiff read the reports ... and he assumed that Newcastle United were going to hold on to him

On October 6 his solicitors wrote telling Newcastle United that it had deprived him and was still depriving him of his livelihood... and was acting illegally in unlawful restraint of trade, and that they were giving Newcastle United a last chance to put him on the transfer list at a non-prohibited (*sic: they probably meant non-prohibitive*) fee.

*

Some observations of the Judge (Richard Wilberforce) during the trial
Extracts from the Weekly Law Report, October 18 1963

... The system of transfer fees was remarkable and unique b
oth within and outside the field of sport...

The transfer system has been stigmatised by the plaintiff's counsel as being a relic from the Middle Ages, involving the buying and selling of human beings as chattels; and indeed to anyone not hardened to the acceptance of the practice it would seem inhuman and incongruous to the s
pirit of a national sport ... (but) one must not forget that the consent of the player to the transfer is necessary (*in fact several cases described in this book suggest that this is not the case:*

that even top players have had little say in their transfer). But on the other hand the player has little security since he cannot get a long term contract, and while he is on the transfer list awaiting an offer, his feelings and anxieties as to who his next employer is may not be very pleasant.

Taking the first question ... does the retain and transfer system unreasonably interfere with the liberty of professional players, after their employment with a particular club has ceased? ... It is considered to be contrary to public policy to restrict this liberty unless the restraint is justifiable in the interests of both parties and in the public interest ...

Do the **retention** *provisions operate in restraint of trade?*

... *(The report describes)* how the system works. The player is engaged by a club under a yearly contract from July 1 to June 30 ... as the year of service draws to its end: (i) he may again be registered for his club between April 1 and the first Saturday in May; (ii) he may, by a notice which must be given between May 1 and the first Saturday in June, be "retained" by his club. The notice of the retention must say what the club offers, which need not be his previous wages; (iii) he may be placed on the transfer list; (iv) if none of these three steps are taken, he is free at the termination of his contract to seek any engagement he can get

Do the retention provisions operate in restraint of trade? The plaintiff claims that they do because they restrict his freedom to seek employment and use his skill after the termination of his engagement. In support of this he cites his own experience in which, after invoking every possible appeal procedure, he was for three months kept out of professional football although he had made it clear that his employment with Newcastle United was not to be resumed. *Here the argument seems to go off track – not least because the original complaint was that his request for a transfer was refused. Eastham later selected a different target for his law suit - the right of the club to hold on to the player (i.e. to retain him).*

The association, the league and the club, on the other hand, say that they do not operate in restraint of trade. They contend that these provisions merely give the employer an option, or a series of options, to extend the contract of employment from year to year and that no question of restraint of trade arises *(But in practice it did if the player did not want to stay and the club would not let him go. As described earlier, there were many high profile cases of the clubs telling players such as Raich Carter, Tom Finney and Jackie Milburn as well as Eastham that they had to stay, even after the end of the years in question. For example, David Jack, the Middlesbrough manager in 1948, told Mannion that even if another club offered a fortune they would not transfer him, saying "Why should we let the best player in Britain go?" Tom Finney faced a similar response when an Italian club tried to lure him away from Preston North End.)*

I (the judge) regard the retention provisions as restrictions coming into operation after the employment has terminated... When the retention notice has been given the player is not, by the effect of it, re-employed by the club; the club has made him an offer and further action on his part is needed before he again becomes employed by the club – he must re-sign ... the Football Association only recognises contracts for a period of a season.

Under the League Rules (1959-60) a player can get no wages until he re-signs, nor does the period before he re-signs count for benefit. That is also what the club was seeking to effect in this case. Over and over again the directors were saying "Eastham must re-sign – unless he re-signs he cannot play for us and we cannot pay him"; this seems inconsistent with the supposition that by the act of retention alone he continued to be an employee (see last paragraph). So I think the retention provisions differ from an option to extend the contact which, once exercised, causes the employee to continue to be an employee, and that **I** am entitled to consider whether, in fact, they operate in restraint of trade.

It seems clear from the evidence that... the retention provisions are used to reinforce a club's desire to secure a transfer fee for a player they do not wish to retain. *(The judge implied that this is unreasonable, but if they have earlier paid a transfer fee for the player surely they should be able to recover some of this fee when he leaves).*

Mr Hardaker, the secretary of the league gave his opinion that the system of transfer fees would not work unless the club had powers of retention ... if a league player is merely on the transfer list, he may escape.

In fact by placing a player on the retain list – possibly at reduced wages – the club with which he is registered can prevent him signing on with any other club. Mr Taylor, a director of Newcastle United, made this plain in relation to a concrete case. He said that this was a particular club who "were willing to transfer him but they retained him because if they put him on the transfer list he might get a free transfer". So the retain list was used to get money for a man they were willing to transfer. *(And why not? The club will usually have paid to have got him in the first place.)*

Mr Lloyd, the secretary of the Professional Footballers Association, ... said he knew of a number of cases of the same kind ... (of) players who have shown quite plainly that they are not going to continue with a club or re-sign with it. Placing them on the retain list does **substantially interfere with their right to seek other employment – and I emphasise this – does so at a time when they are not employees of the retaining club. This seems to me to operate substantially in restraint of trade.**

The pleading *(of Newcastle United and the two organising bodies) s*tates the issue in this way: They say if a professional player would... be at complete liberty at the end of each playing season... to enter into a contract to play for any other football club... the most skilful professional players would be placed under contract by the richer clubs.

(The judge replied) **In my judgement ... the richer clubs - which are to be found in the larger centres of population – already tend to secure the better players**; this is simply because both from bigger gate and money and from the contributions of local supporters of affluence, they enjoy greater resources, and because the best, if not the only way, to use these resources is to buy players with them. It was not established to my satisfaction that any substantial change in this respect would be brought about if the retention system were abolished. On this, as compared with the evidence of Hardaker for the league and Eden for the association, I found convincing the evidence of Lloyd, the secretary of the Professional Footballers Association - a witness who seemed to me more in touch with the realities of professional football, and particularly the considerations affecting the supply and interests of players, than the other witnesses ... He pointed out, first, that it was open to a club which desired to prevent a player from being bought away from it by a richer rival to give the player a longer term contract, and that by staggering the length of contracts clubs could ensure that they could always at the end of any season be left with a nucleus.

Mr Hardaker... went further and said that **if there were no retention system there would be complete anarchy in all world football** *(!!)*, and that the football-watching public in some parts of the country and some parts of the world would soon find themselves without a football club to watch. Mr **Hardaker did not satisfy me that this prophecy of doom is at all realistic**, and further if, as he suggested and as pleading seems to suggest, the contention is that amateur football ...

would be so seriously affected as this paragraph indicates, **I do not accept the contention as proved or even plausible.**

*

The Transfer System
Extracts from The Weekly Law Report, October 18 1963

... Taking this *(the transfer system)* alone – that is, on the assumption that the retention system is not used to reinforce it – it does not appear to me to be so very objectionable.

The case for it is really this. That within the league it provides a means by which the poorer clubs can, on occasions, obtain money, enabling them to stay in existence and improve facilities; and rather more generally that it provides a means by which clubs can part with a good player in a manner that will enable them to secure a replacement *(the judge shows limited knowledge of football here, by not understanding the main reasons for wanting a transfer fee, which are (i) that the clubs naturally want to recover some part of the fee for which they originally bought the player when they eventually come to sell him; and (ii) to cash in on a player they have trained to a high standard.)*

I conclude that the **combined** retention and transfer system as existing at the time of the writ **is unjustifiable restraint of trade ...**

The system is an employers' system, set up in an industry **where the employers have succeeded in establishing a united monolithic front** all over the world, and where it is clear that for the purposes of negotiation the employers are vastly more strongly organised than the employees. No doubt the employers all over the world consider this system a good system, but **this does not prevent the court from considering whether it goes**

further than is reasonably necessary to protect their legitimate interests.

*

> ### *The Verdict*
>
> I grant a verdict against Newcastle United ...
>
> I grant a decision –subject to any necessary discussion as to the form of order – that the rules of the Football Association and the regulations of the Football League relating to retention and transfer of players... are not binding on the plaintiff and are in unreasonable restraint of trade ...

As shown in the box above, the judge, Justice Wilberforce, ruled in Eastham's favour, stating that the retain-and-transfer system was unreasonable (although because Eastham had refused to play for Newcastle, any payment of wages for the disputed period was at Newcastle's discretion).

This ruling had far reaching implications. It entailed that the historic rules of the Football Association on retention and transfer of footballers were no longer binding. The consequence was that all the contracts signed by almost 3,000 members of the Professional Footballers Association were illegal, and the Football League had to modify the system, dispensing with the "retain" elements.

The result was that although Eastham did not gain personally, he succeeded in reforming the British transfer market. The "retain" element of retain-and-transfer was greatly reduced, providing fairer terms for players looking to re-sign for their clubs, and setting up a transfer tribunal for disputes. The "transfer" aspects, however, remained largely unchanged until the Bosman ruling in 1995 and the Webster ruling in 2007.

* * *

Only eight years after Shack wrote his searing criticism of the employment conditions of footballers, his two main aims had been achieved. The maximum wage had been abolished and the clubs no longer had the right to hold their players against their will.

He had been highly influential in pushing through these reforms. On the maximum wage, Jimmy Hill acknowledged the importance of a strong character being willing to stand up and be heard, while others had been unwilling to raise their heads above the parapet. Jackie Milburn, who had also had a transfer request refused in humiliating circumstances, said of Shack "Len Shackleton was a man before his time, not only with his inimitable style of play, but also his foresight into what was happening in the game ... That's why I came to admire Shack more than anybody."

And on the rights of the clubs to 'own' players, Shack had been a crucial intermediary in introducing George Eastham to the financial backer (Ernie Clay) who supported him through the courts.

The only possible blot on Shack's record in those times was his refusal to sign a petition Jimmy Hill had promoted in 1957, in which the players were to confess to having received underhand payments. The aim was to get the facts out in the open in order to pressure the FA and Football League into a full review of the payments system. There were reports that the Sunderland players who were willing to sign regarded him as a scab. But Shack did things his way, arguing that the best way to force progress on all these matters was a players' strike. And history showed that he was right, as the final move that forced the end of the maximum wage in 1960 was indeed the threat of a players' strike. In any case, the confession had proved ineffective with only 40 of the union's 2,500 members signing the document.

20

Freedom at Last:
The Bosman Ruling and Its Consequences

The Bosman Ruling

The Eastman versus Newcastle United High Court Ruling of 1963 had transformed the feudal terms of employment for footballers *in the UK* that had been framed in the nineteenth century. At last it became possible for players, who had previously been owned by their clubs in perpetuity, to leave when their contracts finished.

The landmark decision of the High Court was, in legal terms, that the old 'retain and transfer' system was an 'unreasonable restraint of trade'. It ruled that at the end of a player's contract the player should be allowed to leave if the club did not renew the contract (almost unbelievably this right has not existed before 1963). On the other hand, if a new contract was offered the player did not have the right to refuse if it was at least as good as the previous one. These still left players *to some extent* tied to their clubs.

Later, in 1978, there was a further loosening of the clubs' control over their players. It allowed players the option to refuse the offer of another contract if a new club wanted them, although the new club would have to compensate the old club. Tribunals were set up to determine the amounts payable if the clubs were not able to agree on a fee. Also, players, or their agents, were still prohibited from approaching other clubs to discuss a possible transfer. They had to wait to be approached.

But it took another seventeen years for another more comprehensive court ruling to really open up footballers' employment terms and put the players in the driving seat.

This time the ruling came from the European Court of Justice, whose decisions also apply in the UK. The background to the case was similar to Eastham's. It had started in 1990, when a Belgian footballer called Jean-Marc Bosman wanted to move to another club, the French side Dunkirk, after his contract expired at Liege. At the time clubs were entitled to ask for transfer fees for players whose contracts had elapsed, and Liege attempted to stop Bosman moving by asking for a high transfer fee that was unlikely to be accepted. Even worse, they unilaterally cut his wages and made him play in the reserve team, and later the Youth team.

Within the European Union (EU) freedom of movement is a right guaranteed to all workers: it is one of the four cornerstones of the EU constitution. So Bosman went right to the top, to the European Court of Justice, arguing that footballers should, like everyone else, have the right of freedom of movement within the EU to find work without restriction. More specifically, Bosman proposed that the existing transfer system should be altered so that players whose contracts have expired should be able to move to another club without a transfer fee having to be paid.

The case lasted five years, mainly because there were appeals against each ruling, but eventually reached the European Court of Justice in Luxemburg. Bosman had sued on grounds of restraint of trade, arguing that FIFA's Article 17 was inconsistent with the EU's constitution and therefore illegal.

The court decided - in a ruling in favour of Bosman – that *the existing arrangements did restrict freedom of movement of workers* and were prohibited by Article 39 of the EU treaty of Rome. They therefore had to be abolished. In future no transfer fees should be charged for players whose contracts had expired if they moved to another club within the EU. In effect it gave the players the right to pursue their careers where they wanted; and in practice players from non-EU countries were doing the same. The players were now at last in the driving seat.

But it was what went out with the bathwater that changed the game of football even more than Bosman himself had anticipated. FIFA went further and in a second ruling abolished the 'Quota System' which had restricted the number of foreign players allowed to play for a club. Before Bosman a club playing in the Champions League could field only three foreign players and two 'assimilated' foreign players in a team. But after Bosman clubs were allowed to field any number of players from European Union countries. This second ruling, the ending of the Quota System, was particularly welcome for English teams that had been handicapped by the UEFA ruling that Welsh and Scottish players were treated as foreigners under the "three-plus-two" rule (i.e. that in European competitions clubs could play only three foreign players plus two "assimilated" players who had come through their youth set-up). After Bosman English clubs were able to deploy their full first choice teams, and clubs like Arsenal sometimes fielded teams with no English players at all. Only five years after the Bosman ruling, when Manchester United won the 1999 Champions League final against Bayern Munich, only five of their thirteen players had English nationality.

In the end, though, it was the first ruling - that players could pursue their careers where they wanted - that had an even greater impact on the game. The main consequences were that:

- Players whose contracts had expired and were moving to new clubs started to negotiate higher signing-on fees and wages because their new club did not have to pay the usual transfer fees. And although many players were still transferred while 'in contract', the wage levels of all players was boosted by the particularly high wages conceded to those joining clubs without transfer fees. Some of the high profile players who moved on free transfers were:

    Patrick Kluivert, to Milan, 1997
    Brian Laudrup, to Chelsea, 1998
    Steve McManaman, to Real Madrid, 1999
    Sol Campbell, to Arsenal, 2001
    Jean-Alain Boumsong, to Rangers, 2004
    Michael Ballack, to Chelsea, 2006
    Pirlo, to Juventus, in 2011

- Clubs were no longer able to keep their best players at the end of their existing deals.
- Players still under contracts could ask for better deals by threatening to leave for nothing at the end of their contract if the club failed to accede to their demands.
- As players became more powerful, so did their agents. And they were highly effective in inflating salaries and raising costs even further, in several ways. First, they drove harder deals than their clients, the players. Secondly, the agents were able to insert a new set of costs into the clubs' accounts by introducing out-of-contract players to them, and taking cuts from signing-on fees. Thirdly, they acted as negotiators for the overseas footballers coming into European clubs. Fourthly they advised the clubs as external scouts. And fifthly, they encouraged the players to seek better and better deals. An example was the deal forced though by Wayne Rooney and his agent Paul Stretford, when he won an increase in wages to £300,000 a week after threatening to leave Manchester United to join Manchester City.
- Clubs had to start giving their best players long-term deals to prevent their leaving on a Bosman transfer.
- The smaller clubs lost out because they could no longer rely on transfer fees from selling their talented young players, who could now leave for free at the end of their deals. Also, instead of going to smaller league clubs in the same country for rising stars, the wealthy teams were bringing in 'out of contract' foreign stars. So the funds available to the big clubs were increasingly diverted to the out-of-contract foreign players and their agents rather than going on transfer fees to lower league teams.

Of these consequences perhaps the most important was the first – that after the Bosman ruling the full value of the players who left at the end of their contracts was reflected in costs that *had to be passed on to the fans*. Whereas payments for transfers from other clubs are offset by incomes to those other clubs – *thereby leaving total costs for all clubs combined unaffected* – increases in players' wages *do increase costs*, especially now that agents are involved, and have to be recovered.

So the spiralling wages paid to players post-Bosman meant that the clubs needed more income, and it had to come from the fans. There were two main sources - (i) increased ticket prices for those who attended the games and (ii) charges for the television companies that were showing more and more games for a new set of fans who watched at home or in pubs.

New Fans and New Income: Football Clubs' Revenues from TV Rights

The incomes from television are now well above those from attendance at the matches. Broadcasting revenue accounted for 54% of the Premier League's total revenue in 2015, the highest proportion from any revenue stream in the history of the division.

The two companies that dominate TV broadcasting of the Premier League are Sky and BT.

The success of the leader, Sky, has been highly dependent on live Premier League football since the early 1990s, and the rivalry between BT and Sky has intensified since BT moved into sports broadcasting in 2013 and both bought into partnerships with mobile phone companies. The screening of live football is now so important to both Sky and BT in their rivalry for TV, broadband, mobile and phone customers – what is called "quad play" - that neither of the companies can let itself fall too far behind in the broadcasting of football.

Sky has kept the rights to the majority of matches but the price has been high, as the payments have been bid up by competition between the two media giants.

Sky Sports had an estimated eight million subscribers in 2015 and BT Sport has around five million, many of whom receive the channel free as part of their broadband deal. And the reach of the Premier League is now extraordinary. Staying in hotels from Dubai to Jakarta you can see several live matches most nights of the week.

The Premier League's revenues from the two leading television companies have been negotiated at £5.1 billion over the next three seasons. And the total amount raised when international rights are included is likely to be over £8.5bn over the three year period 2016-19. Also, the BBC is paying £204m to retain the highlights.

Its total incomes now make the Premier League the second most lucrative league in the world, behind the NFL, but having now overtaken Major League Baseball.

The new deals mean that even the bottom club in the Premier League will receive almost £100m a year while the league champions will get over £150m.

These revenues are increasing fast. The two broadcasters will be paying 70% more from 2016 to 2019 than they did in the last three year period, 2013-2016.

Footballers' Wages will continue to Rise

The upward spiral will continue, as increases in clubs' incomes from TV have always been followed by increases in wages.

A few years ago it seemed that the costs of wages were out of control, as even the top clubs were making losses because their super-rich owners were pouring in money in to pay for better players. But today the clubs are more or less back in the black. The English Premier League clubs had record revenues and profits in 2013-14, as payments by TV companies rose and Financial Fair Play rules (see next section) came into effect. A report from analysts Deloitte estimated that combined revenues had risen 29%, and the clubs made pre-tax profits of £187m for the first time since 1999. They suggested that this may mark a turning point in football finance and "a new age" of profitability for top clubs. They observed that:

- The league's wages to revenue ratio – which had been a concern - fell dramatically last year, from 71% to 58%, the lowest since 1998-99.
- England's top division generated over £1bn more in revenues than its nearest rival, Germany's Bundesliga.

- The risks associated with investment in Premier League clubs seem to be diminishing, with future revenue growth already guaranteed through the recently agreed domestic broadcast rights deals from 2016-17 to 2018-19, as well as the success of cost control regulations under the Financial Fair Play rules set by UEFA (the Union of European Football Associations, the governing body of football in Europe).

Deloitte's Sports Business Group also concluded that Financial Fair Play "could be the most significant development in the football business since the Bosman ruling. Early signs are that this is the case. "Indeed the change in club profitability in 2013-14 was more profound than anything we could have forecast." They suggested that with the UEFA Financial Fair Play (FFP) requirements continuing and the Premier League's own Short Term Cost Control measure currently in force for 2014-15 and 2015-16, the wages to revenue ratio should remain close to or below the 60% threshold.

UEFA has said that it is ready to relax its FFP guidelines, but Secretary Gianni Infantino has said that is only because the rules have "proved successful in achieving considerable improvement in the financial health of European football".

In the 2013/14 season in the Premier League:

- Combined broadcast revenues rose by 48%
- Commercial revenue rose by £135m to £884m
- Match day revenues increased by 5% to £616m
- Net debt was down by 6%
- Club wage bills increased by 7%
- Most of the Premier League clubs were making profits

The pattern was similar abroad. In the 2013/14 season:

- In the "Big Five" European leagues - England, Germany, Italy, France and Spain - combined revenues grew 15% to €11.3bn.
- This helped drive the overall size of the European football market to more than €20bn.
- In Spain's La Liga club revenues increased by 3%. (However, all this growth was driven by the two Madrid clubs, Real and Atletico. The other eighteen clubs in the division saw aggregate revenues fall.)
- In Italy, there was only a marginal 1% increase in total revenue for clubs in the top league. Deloitte said that Juventus again demonstrated the commercial benefit - which other Serie A clubs could copy - of investing in, and improving, match-day facilities.
- Germany's Bundesliga saw its revenues rise by 13%, consolidating second place in the big five leagues, driven by a new set of domestic broadcast rights.
- Total Ligue 1 revenues in France grew by 15%, led by a €75m revenue growth at Paris Saint Germain.

There are, however, some threats on the horizon. For example, an increasing number of fans have been streaming Premier League games illegally on the internet. This happens particularly at 3pm on Saturday afternoons, when games are broadcast live in other countries such as Dubai and UK fans access them via online streams. It was estimated that about one million viewers were using these illegal channels every week at the beginning of 2016. The Premier League is trying to get cyber-security companies to block broadcast from other regions of the world, via "geofencing procedures". However, some users are able to circumvent the blocks. Given the large sums that Sky and BT pay for the rights to show Premier League games, most of which is then paid to the clubs, it will be important for the funds available to football clubs to prevent fans using free channels.

Financial Fair Play

Financial Fair Play was first imposed by UEFA, Europe's football governing body, on the Premier League in 2013-14. It had been championed by the now-disgraced UEFA President Michel Platini with the aim of curbing the excesses of the clubs with new super-rich owners who were pouring in previously unknown amounts of money to buy success. The fundamental aim is to make the clubs break even, i.e. to balance their books. But there are also restrictions to keep wages under control.

The rules are very detailed. They cover ninety pages and include rules on paying taxes, wages and transfer fees on time.

The key rules are that:
- The maximum allowable loss is £105 million over a three year assessment period. The ceiling is quite high because UEFA recognizes that many players are on long term contracts and this prevents clubs reducing their costs quickly. But it will be reduced in later years to about two thirds of the initial ceiling
- The maximum allowable loss if the owner did not inject funds is £15 million over three years combined.
- The maximum increase in wages is £4 million p.a. plus any new income from commercial deals.
- Transfer fees are spread (i.e. written off, amortised or depreciated) over a number of years rather than being treated as a one-off payment.

The penalties for non-compliance could be deductions of points, and others yet to be confirmed. The penalties that might be considered are:
- A warning
- A reprimand
- A fine
- Withholding of revenues from a UEFA competition
- Prohibition of registering new players for UEFA competitions

- Restriction of the number of players a club may register for a UEFA competition.
- Disqualification from current or future competitions
- Withdrawal of a title

In practice, the punishments have been very varied so far. Among the strongest punishments were those handed out to the two clubs always likely to be most threatened by FFP -- Manchester City and Paris Saint-Germain. Both teams had been bought by multi-billionaire owners from the oil rich Middle East (Abu Dhabi and Qatar) and received huge injections of funds as the owners attempted to create teams capable of challenging Europe's best. In 2014, both Manchester City and PSG were fined about £50 million; told to reduce their Champions League squads to just 21 players instead of the usual 25; and forbidden to exceed net spending of 60 million euros in the summer's transfer window. Other clubs disciplined during the 2014-15 include Monaco; the Italian teams Inter Milan and Roma, who have also come under new ownership in recent years; and nine other clubs.

21

What Became of the Players who Pushed for Reforms: Shackleton, Eastham, Bosman and Hill?

With Europe's football industry now worth over £20 billion a year and in good financial health, what became of the rebels whose determination had opened up the industry from the controls of the 1950s? In fact, only one of them became rich, as the breakthroughs came too late for the others to benefit much. Their fortunes varied greatly.

Shack

The rebel who had been the most articulate critic of wage control and the 'evil contract' in the 1950s later seemed to have had some reservations - about the eventual explosion of salaries and the domination of the top teams by foreign players, now that they were free to move internationally.

Given his belief that football players were entertainers and that they should be paid, like actors, according to their ability to attract crowds, he might, if he were alive today, have been expected to have approved of the wages paid to players like Messi, Ronaldo, Suarez and Rooney. They could hardly be accused of not being entertainers and it can be reasonably argued that their incomes are justified by the fact that revenues from match attendance and television broadcasts are sufficient to pay these wages.

His limited public statements about today's high wages, however, were not always consistent. In a Radio Five interview in 1996, he was asked if he was envious, and replied "Not really, there are no sour grapes." But in his second book in 2000 his views might be inferred to have changed, from the chapter entitled "Commercially a full circle – from a game with a business in it to a business with a game in it", and his passing reference to 'today's mad celebrity excesses'. On the whole he seemed to have regretted the gap that had opened up between the top teams and lower divisions, and may have felt that things had gone too far.

Rather surprisingly he did not really commit himself in the second book, written just before he died at 78. Instead he quoted *his wife's* view that the wages had become obscene. The rebel of 1955 had perhaps become less outspoken and more conservative in his later years.

Eastham

After winning his High Court case in 1963 George Eastham went on to a have a successful career at Arsenal and just missed being included in the England squad that won the World Cup in 1966. He later went on to become the manager of Stoke City. But 'Gentleman George' was considered 'too nice' for football management, and in 1978 he emigrated to South Africa, where he ran a sportswear business and, as an opponent of apartheid, coached local black children and acted as chairman of the South African Arsenal Supporters' Club.

Bosman

Bosman fell on hard times. In fact his career was on a downward trajectory from the outset. He had been the captain of Belgium's under-21 national team, and was playing for the Royal Football Club de Liège in the late 1980s. But his four seasons there were disappointing, and when his contract expired in 1990, the club offered him a deal at only about a quarter of the $3,000 a month he has been earning and dropped him to the reserve team. Then, after starting his case in 1990, he was out of action for five years until the ruling was made. A year after he won, however, he had to leave third division Vise because he said he could not make a living out of it. He later played in the French second division, followed by a stint in a club on Réunion, an island in the Indian Ocean. Then after a few more brief spells in Belgium's third and fourth tiers, he retired. At 32, he was out of a job, his wife had left him and it was reported that he had moved into his mother's garage.

Meanwhile, his settlement in 1995 had won him £720,000, and a decade later he was reported to have had two houses, one with an outdoor swimming pool, and a BMW. Also, FifPro, the international players' union, had made a further payment to Bosman. He would eventually collect about $1.5 million in compensation from UEFA and donations from FifPro. Bosman was reported to have felt FifPro had not been fair to him, despite its having given him about $450,000 to cover his lawyers' fees and various handouts and finding him a club when he needed a job. Bosman declared the money as gifts, whereas the Belgian tax service considered it income. Before long he owed some $150,000 in back taxes and owned nothing but the two modest houses he had built for himself and his sister.

He was bitter and began to suffer from depression and drink. Bosman's lawyer Luc Misson said: "He gave his career to a court case to serve a cause, but he sees that the transfer fees are still there, quotas on home-grown players are making a comeback and the rich clubs are richer and the poor ones are poorer." (Source: BBC Sport.) But when in later years he returned to Fifpro asking for more assistance the union seems to have taken the view that Bosman would have to take responsibility for his problems. He is now reduced to living off his court indemnities.

Jimmy Hill.

Jimmy Hill took over the baton for the football reforms in 1957. It was the year in which Shack retired and Hill was made chairman of the professional footballers' union, the PFA. At the time he was still playing for Fulham and was aware of what he might have been earning outside football. At his previous club, Brentford, he had, like most footballers, been obliged to take menial second jobs to supplement his modest footballer's wage. Despite having been to a grammar school he worked as a chimney sweep and selling light bulbs.

But over the next forty years he was to have more of an impact on English football than any other individual – first, as a player turned union leader, then as a coach, a manager, a chairman, a broadcaster, a television director and all-round innovator. He even took time out to qualify as a football referee. In his obituaries he was rightly called the architect of the modern game in Britain, football's Renaissance Man.

Even historians who take the view that it is inexorable social trends rather than individuals that shape the course of events would concede that Jimmy Hill at least gave the history of English football a nudge.

Alone amongst the four reformers he became rich from the changes. But he put in at least as much as he took out, transforming the way football was watched, talked about and analysed in England, and attracting millions of new followers.

His first move as chairman of the players' union in 1957 was to intervene in the decisions of a court presumptuously set up by the Football League. This court had handed out indefinite suspensions in 1955 to a group of Sunderland players suspected of accepting under-the-counter payments from their club, and also to the directors involved. Hill succeeded in having them reinstated, and later discovered that the Football League had assumed powers that it did not have.

At the same time, he attempted to flush out the ubiquitous under-the-counter payments to players, to highlight the reality that the maximum wage was insufficient to attract and compensate good players. The approach he chose was a mass confession by the many players who had received them, and he travelled around country to get signatures. But the scheme was a failure, with only a handful of players signing. They did not include Shack who argued that a strike was a better bet - echoing his bizarre attempt six years earlier to get the underpaid Newcastle United team to refuse to play in the 1951 Cup Final just a few hours before it started.

And it was indeed the threat of a strike that eventually resulted in the greatest of Hill's achievements – when he railroaded through the abolition of the maximum wage (see Chapter 8) in 1961. His obituary in the Guardian called it a "profound change that shaped modern professional football".

In the same year, however, he was forced by injury to retire from playing, at the age of thirty-three.

He was not idle for long. Within a few months he was appointed the manager of Coventry City, a club languishing in the Third Division, and bright ideas came thick and fast from the start. He switched the club to a new all-blue kit, renamed the team the Sky Blues and introduced pre-match entertainment, with free soft drinks and snacks for children. He even co-wrote the club song, the Sky Blue Anthem, sung to the tune of the Eton Boating Song. Within two years they were promoted to the second division and in another three years they made the First Division for the first time in the club's history.

But Hill was restless and before Coventry made the debut he had won for them in the first division, he resigned.

In an unexpected career change, he moved into television, starting as a technical adviser to a BBC series. But only a year later he moved on when, apparently to his surprise, he was asked to become head of sport at London Weekend Television. And from that time until today the coverage of football on TV has borne his stamp. An early landmark was the assembling of a panel of well-known talking heads to analyse matches in the 1970 World Cup finals in Mexico. They were Malcolm Allison, Paddy Crerand, Bob McNab and Derek Dougan, and their disagreements and animosity attracted more viewers to ITV than the BBC for the tournament for the first time. And so Hill found that he had invented modern sporting punditry (it was a pity that Shack lived far away in the north). After 1970, the "panel of experts", their post mortems and often self-important verdicts became standard practice in televised football coverage. And this was only three years after he had left his management job at Coventry.

In 1972 he switched back to the BBC to present their new programme, Match of the Day, where he became the joint presenter with Bob Wilson, employing slow-motion replays to analyse highlights such as goals and to examine decisions by referees. The ratings soared to a record twelve million viewers, and he eventually chaired more than 600 editions of the programme, helping to make it a national institution. As a celebrated and much-parodied presenter, he was the first former professional to become the face of football, a trailblazer, as in many areas of the national game, and more forthright in his views than most of those who came before or followed afterwards. His voice still betrayed his origins - his father was a London milkman – and although it had softened it was a far cry from the earlier 'voice of football' the rich middle class delivery of Kenneth Wolstenholme who had so memorably announced that "They think it's all over … it is now" just a few years earlier when England won the World Cup in 1966.

Hill was, however, soon on the move again. In 1975 he returned to Coventry City, first as managing director and later as chairman. In 1981 he converted Coventry's ground into the first all-seater stadium in English football, partly motivated by his slogan, "You can't be a hooligan sitting down." (It was not, however, popular with all the fans.)

Later, in 1987, he returned to Fulham as chairman, and steered them away from the threat of bankruptcy and a merger with Queens Park Rangers. There followed a period of stability and relative success under a new owner, Mohamed Al Fayed, who also owned Harrods. It cemented his place in the hearts of Fulham's supporters, grateful for his success in saving the club from extinction and preventing their beloved ground from falling into the hands of property developers.

During this time Hill also pushed through a key rule change that gave clubs three points rather than two for a win, compared with one for a draw, encouraging teams to play more attacking football. It was adopted in England in 1981, and then all over the world, eventually becoming standard after the 1994 World Cup.

He was also a pioneering influence on the introduction of shirt sponsors, and then team shirts replacing the supporters' raincoats of the 1950s.

How did he achieve all this? Much of it was through the force of his personality. He was a fluent talker and a charmer, but sometimes more than a little opinionated. Self-confident, thick-skinned and dogmatic, his profile was further raised by his appearance. With the bearded jutting chin that he inherited from his mother (the chin, not the beard) he was instantly recognizable and he became a household name. Often parodied, he was loved by many although not by all. Despite being close to a national treasure, Jimmy was said to have worn hostility like a badge of honour. Another pundit, Terry Venables, recalled walking around the pitch at Liverpool with him before a game. Hill had said something critical about the club and the crowd was chanting, "Jimmy Hill's a w*****r". "There's fame for you," said Hill, without a hint of irony. "They love me here." He was not upset to be confronted in cafes by irate members of the public incensed by his forthright opinions on television and gave as good as he got.

His autobiography, The Jimmy Hill Story (1998), acknowledged that he was a serial adulterer during his first two marriages.

He loved his fame. On one occasion, it was claimed that he had failed to notice that his producer had misspelt the word "clock", missing out the 'l', in his last announcement before the credits of *Match of the Day*, reminding viewers to put their clocks back that night. Hill read the script with a straight face, then joined in the hilarity at his apparent slip. Maybe, though, he was well aware of the error before he ploughed on regardless.

Over the years Hill's personality gradually morphed from that of a rebel fighting the Establishment, to an erratic conservative, eventually riding to hounds. He could be pedantic, argumentative and sometimes too pleased with his fame. But he was happy to make fun of himself, and of his prognathic chin, which he had covered up for many years with a beard until he shaved it off for charity.

A short film available with the Daily Telegraph's obituary of Hill shows him at his best. It was recorded on the set of

Match of the Day, and featured Des Lynam, Alan Hansen and Ruud Gullit looking increasingly glassy-eyed as Jimmy spouted on about this and that, much of it about himself. Eventually Hansen had had enough. He rolled his eyes to the ceiling, interrupted Jimmy and said "Jimmy ... will ... you ... just ... be ... QUIET?". He waited a second; then he pressed a button and blew Jimmy up. Or so it seemed. But as the smoke cleared it appeared that Jimmy had survived when his face came into focus again, covered with soot. His clothes were in ribbons; and he was still talking, picking up where he left off "... also, Collymore could break through the Spurs defence at will and ... blah blah blah". The camera then turned to Lynam, who had fallen off his chair with laughter and then Hansen, equally convulsed, and at last to the remains of Hill. He turned ruefully to the camera. "You won't get it better than that" he said.

Not all that he touched turned to gold. In 1976, he won one of the first contracts to bring football to rich countries in the Middle East. It was a great success and he made large profits. But he then made a big mistake; they were reinvested into bringing the game to another non-footballing country, the USA, through a franchise arrangement with a team called the Washington Diplomats. The American venture was a disaster. The league attracted international but ageing stars like Pele and Cruyff, but did not catch on with the American public, and Hill was reported to have lost himself and Coventry some £2 million. His son Duncan told the New York Times "We've lost all the family money. All we have left is our home."

Then in 1996 he admitted having lost another £100,000 in a car business run by two of his sons, and after he was released by the BBC in 1998 he confessed that it was his need to keep earning money that had prompted him to accept a presenter's job with Sky.

Nonetheless, Hill lived in style, owning homes in France, Spain and Sussex. He was given an OBE for services to football in 1994, and a statue of him was unveiled outside Coventry's ground in 2011.

Jimmy headed the ball a lot when playing. This was the old ball, that weighed the same (16 ounces) as the 'new ball' when dry at the beginning of a match. But, because it was not water resistant, it was often twice as heavy by the end of a match played on a muddy pitch. Whether or not this was the reason for the outstandingly vigorous Jimmy succumbing to Alzheimer's over the last eight years of his life will never be known. He died in 2015, aged 87.

The late ITV football commentator, Brian Moore, who worked with him at ITV Sport for many years, said: "If you really want to get in the trenches with someone, get in there with Jimmy Hill."

22

The State Of English Football Today

Summary of the Reforms

English football has been transformed by the changes that were started in the years just after Shack wrote his book. It had been overwhelmingly the most popular sport in the country since the end of the First World War, when the government built Wembley Stadium, and almost 300,000 fans pushed their way through the turnstiles to the first FA Cup played there is 1923. Its capacity was only 127,000. And after that the crowds at English grounds continued to grow year by year until 1948 when they reached a peak, before tailing off[11] and then soaring again when football came to television screens.

But despite the following and the adulation of the supporters, the living standards of footballers had remained pegged to the ground until the reforms of the 1960s.

The story of their subjection was a case study in social history and the depth of British class distinction, snobbery and exploitation. The mediaeval terms of employment imposed on the footballers had been devised as an afterthought almost a century earlier by a self-appointed group with an undisguised disdain for professionalism in sport. They, the Football Association, only grudgingly accepted the need for payment, albeit limited, for football players at the end of the nineteenth century. Their partners in crime were the Football League, the mouthpiece of the hard-nosed local businessmen who ran the clubs as directors. They were as repressive in their own way as their socially superior counterparts in the Football Association. Their interests were in keeping wages low and the players under control - effectively owned by the clubs, and unable to leave if they didn't like them, the town or their bosses. Top international players often lived in temporary housing or digs arranged by the clubs, and travelled to the matches by bus,

---

[11] Source: The Football Manager: A History By Neil Carter, 2006

chatting to the fans, while the directors drove past in their cars. On weekdays the directors could even find their players turning up at their doors as part-time tradesmen. Tom Finney was a plumber and Billy Bingham was an electrician. In fact their lot as tradesmen was in some ways better than that of a footballer; at least tradesmen could change jobs and ask for a rise; and they faced no wage control.

Incredibly, these conditions were not challenged for over fifty years. The main reason was that the players, who almost all left school at an early age, could not find a voice to represent them in a class dominated sport. Whenever they had grievances - over accommodation, requests for transfers or expenses - they were humiliated in boardrooms in which they felt out of place.

The agenda for the reforms was set out in Shack's book, with its withering attack on the players' contract and its litany of telling details - about third class rail tickets for players and first class for directors; the players' receiving less than one per cent of the gate money at the cup finals; and the England players not being allowed to keep their shirts after an international game.

The breakthrough came with the emergence of more articulate players who had been to grammar schools and technical colleges and who eventually drove the reforms through with the assistance of the High Court and the government.

The genie was largely out of the bottle by the early 1960s. But the game did not change overnight. Wages did not rise particularly fast at first and English football was less attractive than, say, the Dutch during the early 1970s. But then English teams came through to win the European Cup an extraordinary six times in succession between 1977 and 1982 (Liverpool three times, Nottingham Forest twice and Aston Villa). There were, however, few foreign players in England until the 1990s, Ricardo Villa and Ossie Ardiles at Spurs being two of the notable exceptions. It needed the Bosman ruling of 1995 to make the game truly international by giving players freedom to move all over Europe.

Where is English football now?

Today football is by far the world's most popular sport. About one billion viewers watched the World Cup Final 2014, equivalent to almost half of the planet's male adult population. In comparison the Super Bowl attracted only 160 million worldwide.

And at club level England's Premier League is the most watched league in the world, with its teams reaching at least the semifinals of the European Championship in most of the last ten years.

The League is now able to attract a large part of the money that the fans are willing and able to pay, with annual revenues around £4 billion – of which 55% comes from TV and 45% from the turnstiles and other commercial channels. Until the 1960s the market was rigged in the interests of the directors. But now, with wage controls removed, the value the fans put on the game is transparent. While many condemn the wages paid to footballers as unfair when compared with those of 'hard working families' the key point they miss is that the hard working families choose to spend their hard earned money to see the football, either at the grounds or on TV.

The game is now truly international, with Brazilian, Spanish, French, African and other foreign stars accounting for two thirds of playing time in the Premier League. And it has vast followings in Asia, the Middle East and Africa.

The quality of the play in England is high, but it has had to draw on the world's talent to achieve this. The best English players - Rooney, Wiltshire, and Gerrard - have never quite made it at international level.

The Premier League is in good financial health. After a period of losses over many years all except one of the clubs were profitable in 2014:

Season	Premier League Pre Tax Profits/Losses
2009-10	-£484m
2010-11	-£361m
2011-12	-£205m
2012-13	-£291m
2013-14	+£198m
2014-15	+£121m

The return of the Premier League to profitability was due mainly to the new disciplinary Financial Fair Play rules that are being imposed by UEFA. Deloitte reported that 19 of the 20 Premier League clubs made an operating profit in 2014, and the League's 'wages to revenue ratio' – which had been a concern – fell sharply from 71% in 2013 to 58% in 2014, the lowest since 1998-99. (It rose, however to 61% in 2015.)

It has been claimed that ticket prices are too high. But attendance at home games for a top Premier League club for a season would cost well under five percent of a modest net income, and 96% of Premier League tickets have been sold in the last five years despite the supposedly high prices. Attendances have risen from 8 million five years before the Premier League started in 1992-3 to 10 million in its first year and 14 million today.

While much of Britain's industry is languishing, football is a great success story. In 2015 the Premier League, contributed £3.4 billion to GDP and more than 100,000 (in terms of fulltime equivalent jobs). It was broadcast to 730 million homes in 185 countries according to the latest statistics available (from Ernst and Young).

The Premier League is also a powerful advertisement for the UK.. You can see English football on TV most nights of the week in most countries (the cricket mad Indian sub-continent being an exception). Somehow we punch above our weight.

The Premier League is the most talked about League in the world. You can get off a plane in Tanzania or Hong Kong and have an intelligent conversation with the taxi driver about English football and continue it with company chairmen later in the day. I recall coming across a tiny village on a dirt road in Sierra Leone where the children were kicking a ball made of rags between the huts wearing old Premier League shirts. Their joyous little faces lit up ecstatically when they heard that we were English and they skipped and jumped as they led us to the hut where they were going to watch a Premier League game that night on a TV fed by a little generator.

The quality of analysis in the press is now exceptional. All the main newspapers employ top quality writers and analysts, and interest in the game has been deepened by the rise of the high profile club managers.

And so is the calibre of football club managers. In his book Shack had dismissed the club managers of the 1950s as "glorified office boys who bow and scrape ... while directors, usually unsuccessfully, perform the managerial functions"; and the managers' apparently unthinking and universal acceptance of the 2-3-5 line-up throughout Shack's time seems to support his judgement of their abilities to think outside the circle. Today, football management is a ruthlessly competitive and highly paid profession, with Pep Guardiola expected to earn £15 million a year on his move to Manchester City; for better or worse, club managers are now international celebrities.

It is not generally known that another of Shack's contributions to the development of football was to kick start the career of England's first great celebrity manager, Brian Clough. Shack - by that time a respected football journalist - telephoned the chairman of Hartlepool United, who were looking for a new manager, to recommend Clough, who had recently retired from playing, for his first job. Clough had no management experience at the time, but went on to win the European Cup twice with Nottingham Forest. In between he was the manager of Derby County, another job for which Shack was the intermediary.

The Counterfactual

WHAT IF the Football League had continued to block all reforms and had succeeded? What if Hardaker – the hard-boiled secretary of the Football League who memorably argued against the 1960-61 reforms by raising the spectre of "the chaotic conditions that had existed before the League was formed in 1888" - had succeeded in retaining his good old days?

In fact there are still many fans who regard the reforms as a Pandora's Box, which has ruined the game. (Pandora was a goddess to whom Zeus gave a box that, unknown to her, contained all the evils of the world. Pandora was told never to open it; but she disobeyed, and all the evils, including death, flew out, leaving only Hope remaining in the box.)

Even Bosman said in retrospect that "Now the twenty five or so richest clubs transfer players for astronomical sums and smaller clubs cannot afford to buy at those prices. So the twenty five pull further and further away from the rest, deepening the gap between big and small. That was not the aim of the Bosman ruling."

Others argue that the clubs have lost their souls; that the players are drafted in from all over the world rather than their local communities; that the big clubs are now too big, while the small clubs will be small forever; that pride in the local football team is dying; and that the big clubs are owned by wealthy foreigners.

There is some truth in all these arguments (see next page). But whatever their validity a moment's reflection would suggest that a strict version of the "without reforms" scenario would seem almost surreal today. Imagine a miserly maximum wage that was still fixed, not by the government but by a committee of cigar smoking businessmen, and teams of players who are tied unconditionally to their local clubs. Few players would want to be professionals at wages pegged at the level of blue collar workers, and those that stood out would probably move to other countries to play. There would be - if Mr Hardaker had had his way - no football on television and no English teams joining what he called the 'wogs and dagoes' in the European Cup.

In practice England would have been sidelined in world football.

The implausibility of such a set up today highlights the extraordinary insularity of the Football League that fought such a brutal rearguard action sixty-five years ago to keep the footballers in their place – and the debt English football owes to Shackleton, Hill and Eastman who resisted them.

Has it gone too far?

Despite the hold English football has on its supporters, there has been much criticism of the less regulated state that emerged out of the reforms initiated by Shack, Hill, Eastham and Bosman. The most common argument is that that the Premier League has somehow lost its soul – in varying ways:

* *The Premier League teams are no longer English, with twice as many foreign players as English players on the pitches on Saturday afternoons.* The big clubs are acutely aware of this, and have invested large sums in academies to nurture local players. But the failures have outnumbered the successes. Manchester United was the last top team to have a team based mainly on players that came through from the youth squad – the class of 1992 (Beckham, Scholes, Giggs, Butt, Gary Neville and Phil Neville). Southampton has also brought through a stream of young players (including Bale, Walcott, Oxlade-Chamberlain and Lallana). But most have failed. Chelsea's Academy in particular had spent a lot, but none of their protégés have made regular appearances on the first team.

Why has England failed to produce enough quality players? Given the following of the game we would expect our English players to be well represented throughout Europe. But they are not, and the English national team's record has been woeful since 1970. After the latest failure in the World Cup a group of English sports journalists toured Europe to discuss the reasons for England's weaknesses with the top managers there, and the consensus was that the English clubs focus on young players' strength, speed and hard tackling at too early a stage. The continentals on the other hand concentrate at first on ball skills and let the fitness, strength and speed come later.

Regrettably, it is difficult to avoid the conclusion that increasing the number of English players via controls on imports would inevitably lower the standard. And the fans, who want results, would not like it.

The linkage of clubs with their local communities - that the Football League and Football Association fought to preserve from the nineteenth century onwards- has been diluted. In Victorian times pride in local teams of local lads in every small town appealed to the atavistic patrician instincts of the Football Association, and it was for this reason that they drew up rules to make transfers between clubs more difficult. Today, however, not only are the players guns for hire, drafted in from all over the world rather than their local communities, but the managers and owners are also foreign. Only the directors and fans are local, and some fans now support the top Premier teams rather than the Darlingtons and Hartlepools. Many Manchester United and Liverpool fans live nowhere near those cities.

But it is the world, not just football, that has changed. Today most of us shop in Tescos and Sainsbury's rather than the local corner shops; and life no longer centres on church youth clubs, dominoes at the working men's clubs and spit and sawdust pubs where all the faces are white. And support for a distant top team is not necessarily less intense than for the local team. Nick Hornby claimed in his book "Fever Pitch" that support for a top football club is the main foundation for feelings of identity of young males today.

The big clubs are now too big, while the small clubs will be small forever and will never be able to compete. This was an argument aired by the FA in the late 1800s: that all communities should have their own club and should be protected from losing all their best players to big clubs.

This argument does not stand up to scrutiny. First, Justice Wilberforce gave it short shrift in his landmark ruling in the Eastham v Newcastle United case of 1963, concluding that the richer clubs - which are to be found in the larger centres of population – will always tend to secure the better players, because of bigger gate money and contributions from affluent local supporters. Secondly, the dominance of the biggest teams has in any case weakened. For years it was always the same four or five - Manchester United, Arsenal, Chelsea, Manchester City and Liverpool – at the top. But it is now wide open. At the time of writing, (March 2016) Leicester City, who were almost bottom last year, are top of the League, Tottenham are second, Manchester United are languishing in sixth place, Liverpool are eighth and Chelsea, last year's runaway champions, are thirteenth. And although teams from London, Manchester and Liverpool are still dominant there are six teams from elsewhere, including Norwich, Stoke, Swansea, Bournemouth Leicester and Southampton, in contention in the Premier League. The reason? The bottom clubs in the Premier League now get two thirds as much from the TV broadcasting rights as the top clubs. They can all afford to buy good players.

* Football *is now just a business.* Even Shack, who argued in 1955 that footballers should, like actors and boxers, be paid in line with the crowds they can attract, had reservations later. In his second book in 2000 he argued that football had come "commercially a full circle – from a game with a business in it to a business with a game in it".

This is undoubtedly true today, with more than half of the top clubs owned by wealthy foreigners, including several from America, where soccer is not the main sport. The owners of all 20 Premier League clubs are listed below.

OWNERSHIP OF PREMIER LEAGUE CLUBS 2015

Club	Nationality of Main Owner	Main Owner
Arsenal	US	E. Stanley Kroenke
Aston Villa	Russian	Randy Lerner
Bournemouth	US	Maxim Demin
Chelsea	Russian	Roman Abromavich
Crystal Palace	English	Steve Parish
Everton	English	Bill Kenwright, Robert Earl
Leicester City	Thailand	Srivaddhanaprabha Family
Liverpool	US	John W. Henry
Manchester City	UAE	Mansour bin Zayed Al Nahyan
Man United	US	Glazer Family
Newcastle United	English	Mike Ashley
Norwich City	English	Delia Smith, Michael Wynn-Jones
Southampton	German	Katharina Liebherr
Stoke City	English	Coates Family
Sunderland	US	Ellis Short
Swansea City	Welsh	Welsh supporters
Tottenham	English	Joe Lewis
Watford	Italian	Gino Pozzo
West Bromwich A	English	Jeremy Peace
West Ham United	Welsh	David Sullivan

Some of the new owners are motived mainly by love of the game (e.g. Abramovich) but others are not.

Are they in it to make profits? There is little evidence. On the contrary they have poured money into their clubs and in general made losses until very recently. And where there are profits they are not very high. The move back into the black does not seem motivated by greed. On the contrary, it is the consequence of the discipline imposed on the owners' profligacy by the new Financial Fair Play rules.

* The *players' pay is absurd*, with no salary caps of the type imposed on US football and baseball teams. It is of course anomalous that footballers are paid huge sums in comparison with teachers and nurses, especially when they can seem undeserving. Often they are portrayed as insubstantial characters, throwing their wealth away on fast cars, tattoos, hairstyling, bling and easy girls, and Shack himself made a passing reference in his second book to 'today's mad celebrity excesses'. The tabloids revel in their peccadillos - Terry's £10,000 tours of Chelsea, Ashley Cole shooting an intern with an air rifle for fun, sex with groupies who see them as gods. But these are in the minority. Arsene Wenger from the start encouraged the consumption of broccoli rather than the beer of Tony Adams's day, and woe betide a young player caught smoking. Alex Ferguson had them all in blazers, allowing only Cantona to turn up in denims. They visit hospitals and crusade against racism. If there is a common problem with footballers it is probably that they have to join their clubs too early to continue their education.

Often they are bracketed with bankers. But they have little in common. We derive no pleasure from the work of bankers and we do not pay them to do what they do (on the contrary, in their unique profession they are able to speculate, not with their money but with ours, and pay themselves bonuses whether they are successful or not). While what is paid to footballers is measure of the pleasure we, the fans, get from the game. The arithmetic is straightforward: if the fans lost interest and incomes from the turnstiles and TV fell by half, the players would be paid only half as much. And vice versa. It is up to us.

Are the players in it just for the money? This suspicion comes often from people not interested in football. I recall the exasperation of my son when he was in his early teens trying to explain to his mother: "Don't you understand? That David Beckham would rather live in a council house and play for England than live in a palace and with a battalion of servants."

* * *

There is at least some truth in much of this criticism. In fact many fans will go on to argue that football is going to the dogs

– that it is has become a business rather than a sport; that big money can buy success; that success comes from paying for mercenary foreign players; that the connections with local communities have gone; and that small local teams will remain small forever.

But if the claim is that football has for these reasons lost its soul they have missed the rhinoceros in the room – which is the uncontestably self-justifying fact that the Premier League is the most watched, discussed and transmitted league in the world, broadcast to almost three quarters of a billion homes in 185 countries in 2015[12]. It has consolidated a hold on the imaginations of supporters not only in England but through all five continents. And, interestingly, it has achieved this despite the facts that its level of skill is not the highest and that the most outstanding players are in other leagues, particularly Spain's La Liga (whose teams have won the European Cup much more often than English teams, see the table at the end of this chapter). But La Liga suffers from predictability: there are only two teams – Barcelona and Real Madrid - that really count; and the same applies in Germany where Bayern Munich dominates, and France where Paris St German has now opened up a gap over the other teams. The English game, however, is much less predictable, with few results guaranteed and the annual excitement over giant killing in the FA Cup. It is contestable, combative and exciting; and at its best - with the high speed, never-say-die commitment of its super-fit players - it can be a glorious gladiatorial spectacle.

The scenes of high drama in English football over the years are embedded in the minds of followers worldwide - Ole Gunnar Solskjaer's goal in the last second to win the European Championship for Manchester United; Dzeko's and Aguero's two extra time goals to snatch the Premier League championship in 2013-14; and Gerrard leading Liverpool to victory in Europe in 2005 by making up a three goal deficit at half time.

By 2016 the Premier League had attracted a truly formidable lineup of the world's best managers – Guardiola,

---

[12] Source: Ernst and Young, The Economic Impact of the Premier League

Mourinho, Conte, Wenger, Ranieri and Klopp. Acccording to Klopp, the crusader for heavy metal football, you don't need to be a Raketenwissenschaftler (rocket scientist) to figure out why they have come: it is that the English league is " the hardest title to win."

The games are watched mainly in pubs from London to Durban to Hong Kong, packed with knowledgeable fans. But to get even closer to the pace, intensity and soul of the game you need a seat in a stadium near the pitch – to see at close quarters the high precision ball control at breakneck speed; to hear the bone on bone impact of the ferocious but overwhelmingly fair tackling; to see the transcendent joy in the eyes of your neighbour as you turn to him after a winning goal; and the shocked empty silence that falls on the ground as an unexpected winner by the visitors lies, static and irretrievable, in the back of the net.

Shack used to argue that footballers were just entertainers, but the reforms he crusaded for have made them much more than that.

Football provides some of the most rousing theatre on the planet, capturing the emotions that religion, patriotism and war gave rise to in the past.

It is not the greed of the clubs, the players, the broadcasters or the businessmen that has brought the money and big business into football; it is the numbers of fans that thrill to the game as it is played today.

WINNERS OF THE EUROPEAN CUP 1956 to 2015

Season	Winners	Country	Season	Winners	Country
2014-15	Barcelona	Spain	1984-85	Juventus	Italy
2013-14	Real Madrid	Spain	**1983-84**	**Liverpool**	**England**
2012-13	B Munich	Germany	1982-83	Hamburg	W Germany
2011-12	**Chelsea**	**England**	**1981-82**	**Aston Villa**	**England**
2010-11	Barcelona	Spain	**1980-81**	**Liverpool**	**England**
2009-10	Internazionale	Italy	**1979-80**	**Notts Forest**	**England**
2008-09	Barcelona	Spain	**1978-79**	**Notts Forest**	**England**
2007-08	**Man United**	**England**	**1977-78**	**Liverpool**	**England**
2006-07	Milan	Italy	**1976-77**	**Liverpool**	**England**
2005-06	Barcelona	Spain	1975-76	B Munich	W Germany
2004-05	**Liverpool**	**England**	1974-75	B Munich	W Germany
2003-04	Porto	Portugal	1973-74	B Munich	W Germany
2002-03	Milan	Italy	1972-73	Ajax	Netherlands
2001-02	Real Madrid	Spain	1971-72	Ajax	Netherlands
2000-01	B Munich	Germany	1970-71	Ajax	Netherlands
1999-00	Real Madrid	Spain	1969-70	Feyenoord	Netherlands
1998-99	**Man United**	**England**	1968-69	Milan	Italy
1997-98	Real Madrid	Spain	**1967-68**	**Man United**	**England**
1996-97	Bor Dortmund	Germany	1966-67	Celtic	Scotland
1995-96	Juventus	Italy	1965-66	Real Madrid	Spain
1994-95	Ajax	Netherlands	1964-65	Internazionale	Italy
1993-94	Milan	Italy	1963-64	Internazionale	Italy
1992-93	Marseille	France	1962-63	Milan	Italy
1991-92	Barcelona	Spain	1961-62	Benfica	Portugal
1990-91	R S Belgrade	Yugoslavia	1960-61	Benfica	Portugal
1989-90	Milan	Italy	1959-60	Real Madrid	Spain
1988-89	Milan	Italy	1958-59	Real Madrid	Spain
1987-88	PSV	Netherlands	1957-58	Real Madrid	Spain
1986-87	Porto	Portugal	1956-57	Real Madrid	Spain
1985-86	St Bucureşti	Romania	1955-56	Real Madrid	Spain

23
Summing Him Up

- It is just possible that Len Shackleton was the most naturally talented footballer ever to play in England. He transfixed the crowd at Sunderland as the best player in 'the team of all talents' for the ten years (1948-1957) he played there.
- But he only played for England five times. A maverick, believing that the point of football was as much to entertain as to win, he would not accept the instructions of the pedestrian coaches of the national team.
- They said he didn't care, but he did.
- He was much loved by the crowds and the players, but he was not always a team player. He did things his way.
- Intelligent and courageous, he put his cussedness to good use, while still playing. A rebel by nature, but one with a cause, he wrote a powerful critique of the state of football, in particular the miserly maximum wage and the exploitative nature of the contract the players had to sign. The terms of employment had been devised in the nineteenth century by group from the upper strata of society who looked down on professional sport. Footballers had suffered and often been humiliated under these rules for over fifty years but few had the courage to put their heads above the parapet and criticize their masters while still employed by a club. Shack did, and was instrumental in the breaking of a sixty year deadlock over wage limits and players being tied to their clubs.
- He did not target the level of wages per se. Instead he made the case that players, like actors, should be paid according to their ability to attract the crowds.
- Within few years of the publication of his book the maximum wage was abolished and players' contracts were reformed. The rearguard action of the FA and the Football League was a case study of English social history and class discrimination.

- It would be going too far to call him the father of modern football but his was the strongest voice for reform before Jimmy Hill took over the chairmanship of the Professional Footballers Association in the year that Shack retired.
- He was not, however, fundamentally motivated by money.
- Nor was he critical of the club where he spent most of his career, at Sunderland. After uneasy periods at Arsenal and Newcastle Shack regarded Sunderland as the best club in football. His critique was aimed more at the two iniquitous pillars of all footballers' contracts nationwide – the maximum wage and the ownership of players by their clubs – as well as the meanness, class consciousness and incompetence of most club directors and England selectors.
- Later he became a journalist, and one with no need for ghost writers or editors.
- In retirement he settled down to family, golf, fishing, a home in the Lake District and winters in Tenerife.

Sources / Bibliography

1. Sunderland Echo, 1948-1958
2. Len Shackleton, 'Clown Prince of Soccer' (Nicholas Kaye) 1955
3. Len Shackleton, 'Return of the Clown Prince'(GHKN Publishing) 2000
4. Billy Bingham, 'Soccer with the Stars' (Stanley Paul) 1962
5. Duncan Hamilton, 'The Footballer Who Could Fly' (Windmill Books) 2013
6. Roger Hutchison, 'A Complete History of Sunderland Football Club' (Mainstream Publishing) (1999)
7. Trevor Ford, 'I Lead the Attack' (Stanley Paul) 1957Colin Malam, 'Crown Prince of Soccer? The Len Shackleton Story' (Highdown) 2004
8. Mick Kirkup, 'Jackie Milburn in Black and White' (Stanley Paul) 1990
9. The Times
10. The Guardian
11. The Daily Telegraph
12. Nick Hornby, 'Fever Pitch'(Riverhead Books) 1992
13. Harry Pearson, 'The Far Corner: A Mazy Dribble Though North East Football' (Little, Brown and Company) 1994
14. Garrincha, press reports and internet
15. Spartacus Educational (Wilf Mannion and History of Footballers' Wages)
16. Gary Imlach, 'My Father and Other Working Class Football Heroes' (Yellow Jersey Press) 2005
17. Eddie Firmani , 'Football with the Millionaires'(The Sportsman's Book Club) 1960
18. James and Barbara Kenyon, 'My Team Manchester United Wrapped Up In the Social History of Football'
19. Andrew Ward and John Williams, 'Football Nation' (Bloomsbury Publishing) 2009
20. The Football Association website
21. Dave Bowler, 'Danny Blanchflower, A Biography of a Visionary', (Victor Gollancz) 1997
22. Law reports
23. Wikipedia
24. Ernst and Young, 'The Economic Impact of the Premier League'
25. Jimmy Hill, 'The Jimmy Hill Story' (Hodder and Stoughton) 1998
26. ESPN.FC
27. Worldsoccertalk.com
28. Salutsunderland.com
29. Readytogo.net
30. Press reports and internet

INDEX

Allison, George 14, 15, 70, 97
Best, George 26, 128
Bingham, Billy 38, 45, 75, 98, 102, 173, 188
Blanchflower, Danny 16, 86-89, 121-124, 142, 188
Bosman, Jean Marc 153-158, 164-165
Brennan, Frank 26, 51-53, 103, 138
Brown, Alan 67, 101, 190
Chisholm, Ken 30, 79, 81, 101-102
Clough, Brian 31, 176
Collings, Sid 79, 102-3
Costa, Diego 8
Daily Express 20, 79, 115
Daniels, Ray 32, 100-102
Davies, George 81, 128
Ditchburn, EW 46, 76, 79-81
Eastham, George 26, 127, 139-143, 147, 151-153, 163-164, 178, 180
Elliott, Billy 81, 100-101
European Court of Justice 153-154
FIFA 69, 154
Financial Fair Play (FFP) 159, 162
Finney, Tom 26, 29, 38, 39, 40, 72, 84, 108, 134, 147, 173
Firmani, Eddie 82, 188
Fleming, Charlie 31
Football Association 45, 50, 55, 57, 69-70, 73, 79-80, 86, 90-91, 132-133, 138-141, 147, 151, 159, 172, 179, 188
Football League 13, 24, 40, 55-58, 79-81, 86, 91, 103, 119-123, 125-126, 132-133, 137-141, 146, 151-152, 166, 172, 177-179,
Ford, Trevor 9, 18, 31, 37, 38, 45, 64, 78-81, 102, 137, 188
Garrincha 39, 105-113
Greaves, Jimmy 37, 73, 128
Guthrie, Jimmy 52, 60
Hapgood, Eddie 70
Hardaker, Alan 79, 119-121, 126, 141, 148-150, 177-178
Harvey, Joe 36, 43, 44
Hazard, Eden 10
High Court 120, 127, 141, 153, 164
Hill, Jimmy 82, 119, 121, 123, 152, 165-166, 169, 171, 187, 188
Hornby, Nick 31, 179, 188
Hurley, Charlie 31
Imlach, Gary 87, 123

Imlach, Stewart 87, 142
Jack, David R. 83
Jubilee Benevolent Fund 58, 91
Lofthouse, Nat 29, 34, 40
Mannion, Wilf 11, 39-40, 51, 84, 134-139, 147
Matthews, Stanley 9, 19, 21, 35-36, 39-41, 68, 70, 72, 76, 92, 108, 124
McKeag, William 50, 53-54, 70, 98
Messi 10, 39, 106, 163
Milburn, Jackie 13, 17, 26, 30, 37, 44, 51, 115, 147, 152, 188
Ministry of Labour 123-126, 140
Mitchell, Stewart 25-26
Morley, Ebenezer 56
Murray, Bill 17, 46, 67, 81, 99, 101, 104
Pele 39, 105, 107-108, 113, 170
Purdon, Ted 31-32, 79, 101-102
Quota system, 154-155
Revie, Don 75, 101-102
Richards, Joe 86, 121-122, 125-126
Rooney, Wayne 55, 129, 156, 174
Rous, Sir Stanley 50, 90-91
Rubirosa, Porfirio 22-23
Schiaffino, Juan 59
Seymour, Stan 16, 48, 52
Shackleton, Len
    Summary of his career 12-20
    Skills 8-11, 35-39, 61-67
    Early life 13-15
    Work in electronics and as a miner 5, 17, 40-41
    Opinions of his peers 35, 39
    Playing for England 68-73
    Personality and friends 96-104
    His book and reviews 11, 19, 59-60, 68, 71, 73, 83-95, 104, 163
    Life after his playing career 114-118
    Assistance to George Eastham 140
    His journalism 11, 20, 53, 115-116, 127, 140, 176
    Family life 85, 104, 140
Shackleton, Leornard Price (father) 12, 96
Shackleton, Marjorie (wife) 18, 60, 92, 98, 104, 116, 164
Sky Sports 157, 160, 167, 170
Stan Cullis 70
Sunday People 115, 135, 136
Swift, Frank 68, 98
Trinder, Tommy 127

UEFA 155, 159, 161, 165, 175
Watson, Willie 62, 63, 74, 100
Wayman, Charlie 17, 18
Wilberforce, Richard 127, 142, 151, 180
Winterbottom, Walter 18, 60, 69-71
Wright, Billy 60, 68
Yashin, Lev 30, 108